WOMEN

Women Studies

Addom.

WOMEN

and a
changing civilization

Winifred Holtby

CASSANDRA EDITIONS
ACADEMY
CHICAGO
LIMITED

1978

Cassandra Editions 1978

Published by Academy Press Limited
360 North Michigan Avenue, Chicago, Ill. 60601
All rights reserved
Printed and bound in the United States of America

Library of Congress Cataloging in Publication Data

Holtby, Winifred, 1898-1935.
    Women and a changing civilization.

    Reprint of the 1935 ed. published by Longmans, Green,
New York under title: Women and a changing civilisation.
    Bibliography: p.
    Includes index.
    1. Women--History. I. Title.
HQ1154.H6 1977   301.41'2'09   77-16373
ISBN 0-915864-28-2 lib. bdg.
ISBH 0-915864-27-4 pbk.

DEDICATED TO

DAME ETHEL SMYTH, D.B.E., Mus. Doc.

AND

MISS CICELY HAMILTON

WHO DID MORE THAN WRITE "THE MARCH OF THE WOMEN."

AUTHOR'S NOTE

I have obtained the material for this little book from a large number of individuals and organisations; but the conclusions that I have drawn from the facts put before me must be regarded as entirely my own. No other person or society can be held responsible for them.

It is impossible to thank everybody who has helped me; but I should like especially to acknowledge the services of the following organisations: The London and National Society for Women's Service; the Six Point Group; the India League; the Open Door Council and the Equal Rights International, and the following individuals: Miss K. Gilchrist, Miss Cicely Hamilton, Miss Vera Brittain, Miss Stella Browne, and Mr. Patrick Brand.

CONTENTS

CONTENTS

WOMEN

INTRODUCTORY

Is there a Woman Problem?

DURING the autumn of 1933 I rode one evening on the top of a 'bus from Rottingdean to Brighton. There were no other passengers except a pretty girl of eighteen or nineteen nestling up against an exuberant middle-aged gentleman in tweeds on the seat before me. His manner was so conspicuous and his voice so loud that it was impossible for me not to overhear his conversation—not, I felt, that he would object to an audience of any size. He was giving his companion a lecture upon foreign policy.

"We ought to show those Germans what won the war," he concluded. "Force. That's the only argument they appreciate. That's what these women pacifists don't understand. I've been in a good many tight corners in my life"—he stiffened his fine shoulders—"and if I hadn't learned to use my own strong arm—well, I shouldn't have been here now."

"But you are here," crooned the girl in dulcet tones. "Very much here, aren't you?"

Whatever her intentions, he took this as a compliment. His confidence increased. As the 'bus rattled towards the long, gabled buildings of Roedean School, he regarded them with frank hostility.

"Awful," he observed. "Imagine a place like that. All those women, cooped up together, scratching each other's eyes out. Women weren't intended for that sort of thing."

"No," cooed the girl. "They were meant to be companions of men, weren't they?"

Her dove-like tones never revealed the docility or satire of her motive.

"I'll tell you what there ought to be," he continued, working himself up into a fine state of indignation. "There ought to be a tidal wave to carry off two millions of them. That would just about level things up. There are too many women. Poking their noses into everything. Too many of them."

I am not going to suggest that the homicidal aspirations of the gentleman on the 'bus were typical of his generation; but it is a matter of common observation that, in the second quarter of the twentieth century, the very existence of women appears to challenge controversy.

No popular magazine considers its appeal to public taste secure unless it advertises symposia on "Are Women Blacklegs?"; "Are Spinsters Superfluous?"; "Is there a Right to Motherhood?" The graver periodicals publish articles on "The Psycho-Erotic Differences between the Sexes," or "The Effects of Industrial Employment upon the Incidence of Maternal Mortality." Novels are written to drive home the conclusion that a woman can or cannot successfully combine marriage and motherhood with professional employment; they are written to prove that "Every woman is at heart a rake"; they are written to prove that wives are more sensitive to emotional reaction than husbands, or that husbands are more sensitive than wives. The Ibsen thesis that women are captives, the Strindberg thesis that women are devils, the Barrie thesis that women are wistful little mothers, the Ethel M. Dell thesis that they are neurotic masochists yearning for the strong hand of a master—all these in different forms transfuse contemporary fiction.

From this conflict of opinion, however, one or two general principles emerge. It is obvious, for instance, that human creatures inhabit a changing world. Four times the ice has crept autumn by autumn towards the equator and four times receded, within the comparatively short period of 550,000 years. Sabre-toothed tigers and mammoths with curling tusks have given way to yoked oxen and the domestic pig. Geography has revolutionised itself, rivers cutting their courses through lakes, fragments of mainland breaking off into the sea and forming islands. Climate and plants and the substance of the earth itself have changed, and man has altered with them. Say what we will of human nature, habits are not what they were. The eyrie perched high in the urban skyscraper may bear some faint resemblance to the cliff-dwelling of Neanderthal man; but the daily occupations of its inhabitants are totally dissimilar. Money and its complexities; government and its preoccupations; sport, organised religion; newspapers; artificial light; quick transport; Black Shirts; Red flags; Tammany Hall; the Vatican and the Icelandic Althing; the Great Wheel at Blackpool and Broadcasting House, provide experiences completely different from any known to our primitive ancestors. And the history of man and his position in the universe has largely been the story of his relationship to this changing world, to the varying phenomena appearing on its surface, and to the community of his fellows who are themselves subject to that law of change.

All popular world histories start with that. "The earth on which we live is a spinning globe," begins Mr. H. G. Wells' *Outline of History*. "The land of Egypt is 600 miles long," opens Mr. Winwood Reade's *Martyrdom of Man*. Van Loon's *Story of Mankind* is philosophic rather than geographical in its primary observation: "We live under the shadow of a gigantic question mark. Who are we? Where do we come from? Whither are we bound?" The more ceremonious Buckle, writing at a time when serious subjects were taken seriously, preludes his *History of Civilisation* by the optimistic remark that: "Of all the great branches of knowledge, history is that upon which most

has been written, and which has always been most popular."
And so they go on. Man, it appears, is concerned with the
world he inhabits, its geological structure, with his own
existence and with his study of these affairs. His problem
is his relationship to the universe.

But when the inquirer opens the volumes dealing with
women, he enters at once a different world. Supposing he
picks up *A Short History of Women* by John Langdon Davies
and seeks enlightenment from the synopsis of the first
chapter. It begins: "To understand the history of women
we must begin by asking ourselves the meaning of sex in
the universe. What is sex? And why is sex?" *The
Evolution of Woman* by G. W. Johnson strikes another note.
"Many have sought to discover the eternal feminine by
wandering over the fields of biology, and from flowers,
bees, birds and other beasts, including human beings, have
drawn imaginary pictures of ideal womanhood." The
titles become more challenging, more controversial:
*Woman's Dilemma; The Woman Problem; The Woman's
Side*.

The historians of woman take it for granted that she is
primarily concerned, not with geography, but with
biology, not with philosophy, but with personal morality
and ideal character. Man's problem is his relationship to
the universe, woman's they suggest, her relationship to
man. . . . "He for God only; she for God in him. . . ."

So widespread and dominating is that notion, that only
by a strong effort of will can we remember that women
also may seek some answer to the ultimate questions of the
good, the true or the beautiful; that they also are affected
by climate, wealth and government; that pleasure may
attract or pain afflict them; that, in short, the only adequate
history of women would be a history of humanity and its
adventure upon a changing globe.

Why that effort of will is necessary, why the whole subject should appear so enormously controversial, why the

phrases "sex war" and "sex antagonism" should occur so frequently in its discussion; why we are constantly vexed by appeals for Women's Rights, Women's Wrongs, and Fights for Women's Equality, as though life for a woman were one prolonged campaign, why the gentleman on the Brighton 'bus should have been so indignant, together constitute a social problem which it is impossible to ignore.

At this time we are living through one of its recurrent crises. During the past hundred years, the position of women radically altered. A new attitude recognised their common humanity as of greater importance than their sexual difference. Doors that were shut, opened. Occupations once forbidden were permitted. Interests formerly exclusive were shared. Most important of all was the new self-respect and assurance of equality achieved by women themselves.

In a few countries of Western Europe, in America and in Russia, a generation of women grew up with little knowledge of the old impassable division between "man's place" and "woman's place." The notion of "sex antagonism" seemed ridiculous to boys and girls who, in Sweden, Holland, Germany or England, attended the same, or parallel, schools, took the same examinations, entered upon the same technical training, walked together, played together, read, argued, studied, lazed and laughed together, even dressed in fashions not dissimilar for the sports that were their common amusement. The attitude of the nineteenth and pre-war-twentieth-century "feminist" seemed incomprehensible to them—something unnecessary, exaggerated and more than a little ugly.

But that again is changing—indeed, has already changed. Last year I received a letter from a woman, personally unknown to me, describing a situation which I think is not unusual:

"Within my family of one son and two daughters," she wrote, "there has never been any suggestion that the

girls were debarred from any form of activity for which their quality and courage fitted them.

"If the question of 'sex qualification' arose, we dismissed it rather casually as being unimportant. With the result that my daughters, now 26 and 24, have not shown any strong pro- or anti-feminist bias. They had no need for strong opinions, as they did whatever they wanted to or could do, the complete acceptance of women as human beings being taken as a matter of course. Suddenly now the younger and unmarried one (who is now throwing herself into organising work of a semi-public nature) begins to react to something 'in the air' which points to a felt need to defend her status.

"I consider her fairly representative of the more serious and capable young modern girl, although for her period she has had greater freedom than some. In her case this new tendency can be traced to a threat of reaction on the part of men—not of her own, but the younger war generation. She finds men whose outlook she respects beginning to talk of what women should and should not do, and inclined to stress their value as women in a more restricted sphere than men. [That this seems unusual to her, interests me and reminds me of how much has been gained.] The effect on her is expressed by a reluctant admission that though she has never thought of herself as a militant feminist, and would 'hate to be,' she feels a militant and protesting spirit rising within her: and this seems to me a deplorable setback. As this feeling has sprung up in an environment decidedly more Left than Right . . . I can only account for it by its being due to something that is 'in the air.' "

That letter, expressing the doubts and misgivings of a woman of the generation which saw the struggle for the enfranchisement of women and its victory, a woman who brought up her children on the assumption that the victory was secure, and who now sees the position again challenged,

6

seems to me typical. The same uneasiness is being constantly if less coherently expressed in hundreds of normal and not specially "politically minded" households to-day. We hear it in girls' schools, in shops and offices. A sense of bitterness infects many public utterances, speeches and articles, made on the subject of women's position in the state. The economic slump has reopened the question of women's right to earn. The political doctrine of the corporative state in Italy and Germany has inspired new pronouncements upon the function of the woman citizen. Psychological fashions arouse old controversies about the capacity of the female individual. The problems which feminists of the nineteenth century thought to solve along the lines of rationalism, individualism and democracy, present new difficulties in an age of mysticism, community and authority. So that in 1934 the recurrent riddles are repeated; is it an error to demand for men and women equality of opportunity in every field of human action? Was the feminist movement a mistake? Are women human beings, and if so, is the bond of common humanity stronger than the division of sexual difference? Have we to readjust our ideas all over again? And whither, in 1934, are women going?

CHAPTER I

HARDLY HUMAN

HERE, at least, are the recurrent doubts, the questions, the controversies. Have they always existed? If so, what started them? Are they part of that natural exclusiveness which from time to time leads groups of individuals— a class, a nation, a race—to deny full humanity to all those who do not comply with an arbitrary set of qualifications— which makes the white settler in Kenya incredulous of the humanity of Kikuyu, or the Aryan German disinclined to accept the humanity of a Jew? Or does sex-conflict derive from something more fundamental? What is its history?

To answer such questions adequately, we should be forced to re-tell the whole tale of human life upon this planet; but while avoiding that, it is possible to trace back to their historical origin certain traditions and convictions which have dominated the position of women; to discover why, during the past hundred years, these theories lost their power, and why at the present time they have been at least partially revived.

In doing that at once we find ourselves confronted by the enigma of the Primitive Community.

Weakness and Mystery

Primitive Communities have provided one of the happiest hunting-grounds for the human imagination. Knowing so little for certain, we can make the few accepted facts fit almost any theory. Our earliest forefathers kept no records; we can only guess their story by the rather hazardous procedure of observing the behaviour of the

8

most primitive peoples still surviving or of reconstructing some human background from the archæological remains, bones, arrows, or axes, presumably remaining from those periods.

Reconstructing the conduct of a society from skeletons and broken pottery is rather like guessing the probable setting and plot of a village play from properties dropped and noises made behind the scenes before the curtain rises —an attractive pastime, whose results are not, however, to be taken too seriously. It is not surprising, therefore, that we have almost as many different interpretations of the story as there are books written about it.

But when one, all or none of the theories have been adopted, there remain two or three facts about women's position in that early world which seem probable enough and are widely enough accepted, to be of some use to us.

We do not know whether, as a general rule, male and female hunted together, played together, together guarded the cave, picked berries and drove away intruders. Probably, as to-day, local custom differed. But it is obvious that while women were pregnant or nursing their children they would become physically handicapped in a society where agility, muscular strength and endurance were at a premium. Yet just at the time when they were least able to hunt or fight, they would be making that special contribution to the group without which it could not continue —the gift of new life. It would therefore be necessary to protect the creatures—necessary, yet tiresome. It seems as probable as any of these conjectures can be, that with the necessity for protection first arose the element of contempt in men for women—of that patronage which is bred from solicitude.

But with patronage for the protected and contempt for the weak went awe of the inexplicable. It seems clear that from very early times women were regarded as a peculiarly potent source of magic. Mysterious things happened to them—physical—periodicity, so much more evident in females than in males, pregnancy, child-birth and lactation. How did they happen? Why? Nobody knew—certainly not women themselves. All mysteries alarm minds groping between the physical and the supernatural; and if throughout history masculine superstition has regarded a woman as a mixture of goddess, witch and devil, this is doubtless a legacy from the age when her predecessors accepted this estimate of themselves.

The element of magic has had another effect on women. One of the oldest beliefs of which we know is that the man who touches the person or possessions of another, or even in some cases, crosses his shadow, may be infected by that other's quality. The doctrine of sacramental eating of the dead, which figures crudely in certain forms of cannibalism and with infinitely greater refinement in the Christian Mass, is a further development of the same idea; but we can see how the theory could act when applied to touching a menstruating, a pregnant or a nursing woman. The man who touched her or her possessions would believe himself to be infected by her weakness. Her curious condition might invade him. The woman must keep away; she was dangerous, unclean. So, it seems probable, arose one of the superstitions which has, throughout its entire history, done most harm to women. It survived in the cult of uncleanliness, which runs through pagan custom and Hebraic law, and which affected the attitude of the early Christian Fathers and still influences many men in their thoughts about women. It surrounded with an atmosphere of mystery and morbidity the common physiological operations of the female body. It handicapped research, impeded the growth of medical knowledge, and for centuries hedged about the whole subject of childbirth, its antecedents and results, with a high barrier of folly, ignorance, and blinding prejudice. The suffering of child-wives behind the Indian purdah, the maternal mortality rate to-day in Europe, the grotesque mixture of sentiment, outrage and disapproval still impeding the application of justice to women's economic activities, are all indirect consequences of that pagan fantasy.

Enter the Ladies

When first we learn human history from direct record, we are confronted by the River States of Babylon, Assyria and Egypt, and by forms of civilisation in which women appear to have played a specialised but often quite dignified and influential part. The Babylonian Legal Code preserved to us in the Laws of Hammurabi, 2,350 B.C., suggests that the relation between men and women, especially in the laws of marriage, was not so different from what it is to-day in Europe. Marriage was monogamous—except when a childless wife might offer to her husband a female servant who could bear him children. Husbands were bound to support sick wives. It is evident that able-bodied women were capable of economic independence. Widows could take their husbands' place and property; women could be scribes, elders, judges and witnesses; but, as to-day, husbands were responsible for their wives' debts, and—unlike to-day—adulterous wives were drowned unless their husbands agreed to forgive them and the king pardoned their delinquent lovers. The temple system too, found room for priestesses, with considerable influence and property. If, at the bottom of the ladder, were captive slaves, at the top were independent and active women.

We know too that the religion of these riverside settlements and cities included a worship of fertility. There were Mother Goddesses: Ishtar in Babylon, Astarte in Phœnicia, Isis in Egypt. Reverence for these must have induced respect for motherhood, and a more adequate recognition of women's biological contribution than the vague terrors of revulsion from uncleanliness felt in more primitive societies.

In Egypt, where life was even more secure and culture more elaborate, among the farms by the Nile and in the cities, women achieved even greater legal advantages and social freedom. We know that they governed; on several occasions the empire was ruled by queens such as Nitocris, who lived about 2,475 B.C., and Sebek Neferu Ra. The fine intellectual beauty of the idealised portrait of Princess Nefert who lived six thousand years ago, reveals a subtly civilised quality of pride and self-assurance. Hatasu, royal heiress and sister-wife of Thatmose III, shared the sovereignty with him for fifteen years or more, and proved so much the senior partner that when she died her husband-brother-consort, reacting violently against her domination, defaced all monuments to his departed wife. On the other hand, the heretic king Akhnaton is believed to have been devoted to his wife, and was frequently sculptured with her seated beside him in his chariot, and once, with charming informality, on his knee.

But beyond the royal ranks, women could hold property. Marriage contracts survive, giving wives complete control of the joint estate. Concubines and wives of rich men, merchants, farmers, elders and scribes seem to have shared each other's interests and responsibilities—male and female, husbands and wives alike. As in Babylon, priestesses secured peculiar privileges, evolving a discipline adapted to their own vocation rather than to standards imposed on them by masculine values. Again as in Babylon, slaves, male and female, were at the mercy of their proprietors, although certain rules have been discovered purporting to regulate their position.

But during the later years of the Egyptian civilisation a new social phenomenon appeared. As life became more secure, the women of the wealthier families were required neither to labour nor to fight. Childbirth and suckling were not for them perpetual occupations. Their husbands or lovers appear to have regarded them, not as sources of labour, but as opportunities for display. The first evidence of using leisured ladies as a means of conspicuous consumption appears among that subtle slave-owning culture of the Nile, and a rough logic of historical development, to be repeated in varied forms at different periods, asserts itself.

When a pioneer community is still insecure, constantly forced into conflict by war-like neighbours, it is necessarily dominated by military values. Woman's function then is to give birth to fighting sons and provide comfort and recreation for the tired warrior. She may be brave, agile and tireless—admirable qualities in guerrilla warfare; but she is handicapped by muscular inferiority, and by her far more disabling liability to become, at however inconvenient a crisis, pregnant. Her helplessness at childbirth, her preoccupation with the child she suckles, are crippling handicaps during a campaign, and her biological characteristics tend to make her more interested in the preservation than in the destruction of life—(though women have been merciless enough, goading on warriors from the housetops, mutilating the wounded, robbing the dead). Still, in military societies it is inevitable that they should occupy a subordinate position, taking their orders from the planners of aggression and defence, though within their limited domestic sphere they may exercise fairly strong and liberal powers.

When the community becomes more stable, it may relax its discipline but does not necessarily replace its values. The cities of Babylon, Agade and Thebes had security enough in which to develop a luxurious and sophisticated urban life; certain women who lived there achieved considerable power and almost complete freedom of action; they acquired the graces, prestige and indirect influence that ladies have exercised in all civilised communities; but this freedom accompanied loss of essential occupation. To play the part of an additional ornament to success is not adequate life-work for an adult human being. The legends of Egyptian decadence foretell with exotic exaggeration the tragi-comedy of Shaw's *Heartbreak House.*

The Greeks had a Word for Them

When we come to the Mediterranean civilisations, the cycle repeats itself.

Knossos is a riddle—the puzzling chard of a completed thing, of which we know neither the beginning nor the end. From its fragments we may deduce that while our own ancestors, dressed in skins, painted with woad, scrambled grubbing for roots in their barbarian forests, the small sunlit isle of Crete was piled with blocks of city flats, with bathrooms, hot-water pipes and other modern conveniences; that merchants brought to them wares from all the Mediterranean coastline; that women wore corsets, designed elaborate flounced dresses, drank from cups of delicate workmanship, and corresponded in an intricate system of hand-writing; but what they told each other, what freedom of action and dignity of status they enjoyed, what part they played in the life of the community, remain unknown.

The story of Greek experience is more discernible. Again it follows in its main lines the broad curve of the River civilisations; but the details are not simple, and the higher development of male intelligence made the results of cleavage more unfortunate.

There was a time, if we can judge from Homer, when women's lives were free and dignified. Society centred round the large households of prominent men, as in medieval Icelandic or ancient Hindu custom, and sometimes these households were controlled by women. Penelope in the *Odyssey* took charge of affairs during her husband's absence, Nausicaa had to ask her father's leave for the wagon in which she rode to wash her clothes and bathe; but it is easy to see that their relationship was one of mutual affection and respect; the girl's frank and courteous attitude to Odysseus is significant; and it was her mother Arete to whom she directed the stranger's supplication, if he desired hospitality in Phæacia. Like the Hindu women of the *Rig-Veda*, these girls and mothers of Homeric times, living in an armed pioneer community, frequently exercised authority for fathers and husbands absent at the wars. The same was true of the Lesbians of the seventh century B.C. When their men sailed away, adventuring, trading and fighting, the women at home exercised an authority which they never afterwards entirely abandoned. The great ladies in medieval castles enjoyed similar responsibility while their husbands were engaged upon crusades or territorial feuds.

It was in the comparative security of the city, Athens, that the shadow of ladyhood again fell across the position of women. As in Egypt—to a smaller extent, and in Lydia to a far greater one—passion and possession dictated emotional motive; tradition, developed during a military period, dictated social values; the liberality of the Homeric household degenerated into something more closely resembling the purdah or harem ideal. "A free woman should be bounded by the street door," declared Menander. "My duty," said the wife in Xenophon's *Æconomics*, "is simply to be modest." One is reminded of the sensibility of the eighteenth-century miss. The awakening of intellectual life which glorified Greek civilisation passed over the heads of ladies sitting at home among their servants, their embroideries, their pat-ball and girl-children. Boys were taken from them as soon as possible; they were neither adequate guardians for their sons nor desirable companions for their husbands. Their functions to serve, to amuse, to adorn became so specialised that they could no longer adequately serve, nor entertain, nor decorate. Their husbands sought more congenial companionship among the educated Hetairæ, women of culture and independence who belonged at least to a *demi-monde*, whereas the unfortunate wives belonged to no world at all, but only to their husbands' hearth and bed.—(Not even to their board, for, leading such sequestered lives, they became too dull even to take part in the discussions following banquets which, however much idealised by Xenophon and Plato, still must have contributed largely to the intellectual activity of the age.)

Their final state is summed up in the bitter cry of Euripides' Medea. "Of all things that have life and sense we women are most wretched, for we are compelled to buy with gold a husband who is also, worst of all! the master of our person. And on his character, good or bad, our whole fate depends. For a man when he is vexed at home can go out and find relief among his friends or acquaintances; but we women have none to look to but to him. They tell us we live a sheltered life at home while they go to the wars; but that is nonsense. For I would rather go to battle twice than bear a child once."

That may be special pleading. Medea was not Every-woman and Jason certainly no candidate for the Dunmow Flitch; but the protest was no less sincere and urgent. Take from a woman the necessity and even the possibility of a full day's work; take from her all opportunity for intellectual development, for exercising her responsibility as a citizen, for meeting her contemporaries, for serving a cause, pursuing an art, or even sharing the activities of her husband, and what can she do? She held no property; she practised few domestic crafts; she could not even exercise her ingenuity as a hostess. Pericles, in his perhaps over-celebrated Funeral Oration, observed that women "should not belie their womanly nature, the great glory of which is that they should be as little as possible spoken of amongst men, whether for good or ill." Women only existed, as it were, on suffrance, their chief duty, to be seen as little as possible and not heard at all—hardly even, in fact, noticed by the men who were their masters.

In Sparta conditions were different and more tolerable. At the time of the city state's most vital growth, when it imposed upon itself a discipline comparable to the sternest dreams of German Nazi, Italian Fascist or Russian Communist to-day, woman's place was estimated according to military values. But even though regarded mainly as good breeding-stock for warriors, women were encouraged to train their bodies in athletics; naked girls drilled with boys in the gymnasia; outside marriage free love was widely tolerated, and women as well as youths were considered to be proper objects of romantic passion. Men were expected to marry and produce large families, the children of which were taken before a committee of hygiene. Spartan mothers, whatever restrictions might be laid upon their activities, had at least a vital function in the state. They were not shut away, like the Athenian ladies, with mirrors, cosmetics and chit-chat, to devise a technique for passing time without spending it.

There were protestants in Greece against this lethargy of life for ladies. It is true that the political theory of the day found nothing wrong with a system which deprived the state of the active co-operation of half its citizens, a deprivation observed by the French political theorists of the eighteenth century with considerable effect upon the future of women. Athenians, accepting as natural a state of economic slavery for one class, found nothing unnatural in the lack of social and psychological freedom for one sex. It was not the statesmen so much as the artists and philosophers who revolted. Plato in his *Republic* gave equal civil rights to men and women. Socrates was able to impress even the bluff and anti-feminist soldier Xenophon so much that in his version of *The Banquet* he records the philosopher's remark that the agility of the little dancing girl almost persuades him that women might be the equals of men save in muscular strength and stability of judgment —(a remark which to-day sounds tepid enough, but

17

which to Xenophon must have been revolutionary). It was Euripides who made the outcry of women articulate in the *Medea*, and who in *Alcestis* made a husband's acceptance of his wife's sacrifice seem rather comic and ignoble. Aristophanes mocked male superiority. Praxiteles, designing his superb and queenly Venus, and the creator of the proud, serene asexual Athena Parthenos who stands, with helmet and shield, her entire aspect conveying neither masculinity nor feminality, but a human incarnation of divine intelligence—such men must have dreamed of a world in which women fulfilled a prouder purpose than respectable and compulsory parasitism. We cannot tell how far the women, sharing their aspiration but less skilled in those arts which make the protest survive the protestant, cried out against their lot and tried to devise a more honourable social pattern for their lives. We only know that if such an attempt were made, it failed. For throughout all ages the rebels are in a minority. In ancient Greece, too many circumstances were against them.

It is significant that the history of Macedonia provides us with only one full-length portrait of a woman—Olympias, the mother of Alexander the Great, a princess of Epirus. And she is one of the tremendous evil figures of legend—ambitious, spiteful, jealous, superstitious, probably responsible for her husband's murder, certainly responsible for a large part of those extravagances which turned her son's genius to disaster. She was at once a portent and a vengeance, a sign of the lengths to which prohibition from legitimate action can drive an energetic woman, a retribution to society for the degradation of her sex.

Mothers in Israel

Meanwhile during Egyptian exile and pioneering periods in Asia Minor the elaborate mechanism of Hebrew society was taking shape. Before their exile, a father from the Ten Tribes could sell his daughter as a slave or concubine;

he had the power of life or death over his children. In that nomadic life then, as to-day, women were physically at a disadvantage. Pregnancy, nursing, and muscular inferiority placed them under the power of men, and, in spite of notable exceptions, of women who became judges, women for whom their suitors were willing to serve seven years, women who, by adroit practice of the arts of assassination, gained signal patriotic honours—in spite of these, the mothers in Israel were heavily disciplined. Their heads might not be uncovered before strange men; with minors and slaves they could not form the quorum of ten required for congregational worship; above oxen but below houses, they might not be coveted as possessions, according to the commandments of Mosaic law. The pagan doctrines of uncleanliness and purification passed into the social concepts of Hebraic custom. All through Leviticus we find them underlying the whole regulation of sex, marriage and maternity.

The liberating tendency of Christ's teaching broke through these, as it broke through other codes of law. His contemporaries were obviously puzzled by a man who made friends with women as though they were His intellectual equals, discussing with them His philosophy, accepting their intimacy, refusing to condemn breaches of sexual morality as though they were the most serious of all sins. Whatever attitude the Christian Church was later to adopt towards women, there is no question that its Founder recognised them as human beings, and treated their spiritual individuality as of greater importance than their sex.

The results of His influence would almost certainly have been more immediate and more radical had it not been exercised upon a people as profoundly convinced of woman's subhumanity as the Hebrews, and had the organisation based upon His teaching not matured within the borders of the Roman Empire.

Roman Matrons

We know little enough of the early Italian civilisation of Etruria. Etruscan remains, vases, tombs and urns have preserved for us fragmentary pictures of a vanished culture so gay, so fresh, so jocund with vivid happiness that twentieth-century artists like the late D. H. Lawrence have woven round them a charming fairy tale. Etruria to them glows like an earthly paradise, where golden-haired courtesans disported endlessly with merry gentlemen at delightful meals; where girls and boys danced for simple erotic pleasure among the cypress trees and olives, where life was rich with direct intuitive experience. It is all possible, but until our knowledge increases we cannot tell whether the urn-painters gave a more complete representation of Etruscan reality than might be found by a stranger who knew no more of modern English life than he found on posters advertising travel on the underground railways. There too are smiling blondes inviting young gentlemen to idealised meals, processions, pageants, parks and carefully selected architectural beauties. Etruscan women may have been no happier than the girls of Coney Island or Hampstead Heath.

The Romans themselves, with their genius for order and codification, reduced the patriarchal tendencies of Mediterranean and Semitic civilisations to the rigid law of *Patria Potestas*. Fathers, as in the early Hebrew days, had rights of life and death over their children, women were in perpetual legal tutelage, their husbands after marriage assuming the power held previously by their fathers. They had no rights of citizenship, could exercise no civil office, make no contract, bear no legal witness, nor choose their own domicile. Their husbands were their proprietors—hence the enormous emphasis laid upon physical chastity underlying the story of Vergilia, slain by her father to prevent a fate reckoned worse than death, or the legend of Lucrece, who stabbed herself as the only adequate response to rape.

This dominance by husbands and by fathers, this legal submission, this immense emphasis laid upon sexual integrity, were not imposed upon cowed and unwilling women. There is ample evidence that they, for the most part, accepted freely the standards of their time. Some were rich, and it was not only against adornment by uxorious husbands with a taste for conspicuous consumption that in 215 B.C. the Lex Oppia forbade to women the wearing of more than half an ounce of gold, or ostentatious furnishing of carriages.

It was, indeed, this sumptuary law which aroused the Roman matrons to their most energetic political action. They had no constitutional rights of protest, but Livy describes their canvassing of votes, and their system of picketing the houses of leading supporters of the Bill. Cato the Consul, a Puritan mysogynist, anticipated the remarks of his nineteenth-century successors when he observed: "If women had only a proper sense of shame they would know it was not becoming in them to take any interest in the passing or annulling of laws. But now we allow them to take part in politics. If they succeed, who knows where it will end? As soon as they begin to be equal with us, they will have the advantage over us." The words appear oddly familiar.

It is not quite irrelevant to remember that this same Marcus Porcius Cato secured the expulsion of Manlius from the Senate for the crime of kissing his wife in daytime in the presence of her daughter. The Consul appears to have shared with Strindberg and other celebrated mysogynists an exaggerated suspicion of the domestic affections.

But in spite of the laws, in spite of Cato the Consul, the Roman civilisation produced remarkable women—Cornelia, the mother of the Graccii, Volumnia mother of Coriolanus, Calpurnia, the younger Pliny's learned and loving wife. A society founded upon military strength and political power, for which they had no training, prevented the full development of their personalities; but they were not, like their Athenian predecessors, devoid of initiative; within strict limitations they exercised social, domestic, and even cultural influence. And when, with the decline of the empire, came a sense of increasing insecurity and lack of belief in life, their refusal to have children was possibly one of the several reasons contributing to the weakening of Rome before the barbarian invasions.

It was this sophisticated yet patriarchal society which the new doctrine of Christianity invaded. It came preaching that God was no respecter of persons—neither male nor female, bond or free; that individual souls were equally important in his eyes; that God was a spirit, and that the flesh, and all its impedimenta of sex distinction and muscular superiority or inferiority, were of secondary importance. It told of a Founder, who had formed intimate friendships with women; it was supported by an organisation in which women themselves—Lydia, Damaris and Priscilla—had played a prominent part.

All this was to the good, and it seems clear that during the first Roman Christian period, before the official conversion of Constantine, women were among the most enthusiastic converts. Here was a way of escape for them from the limitations imposed by their own physical structure and the advantages which men had taken of it. Here was a rational foundation for that self-respect which many had felt instinctively, and for which hitherto only the Stoic doctrine had supplied any adequate intellectual justification. Here was a philosophy encouraging those instincts for the preservation of life, for love, for constructive security, which found little expression in the social code of a military empire. So women partook of the common meals, served as deaconesses, "spoke with tongues" in congregational worship, and later on, faced martyrdom with equanimity. To them, as to slaves and outcasts, Christianity was a faith worth dying for.

But that simplicity of spiritual enfranchisement could not endure. It became entangled in the elaborations of ecclesiastical philosophy. Three converging influences destroyed its original liberality. To the Roman code of *Patria Poestas* was added the Mosaic doctrine of women's uncleanliness and subordination. These intellectual conceptions and social traditions were lent emotional intensity by the passionate preoccupation with the body, its rapture and its vileness, which came from the desert countries and reacted with irrational violence upon the position of women. It found its most striking Christian expression in Tertullian's bitter cry: "The sentence of God is on this sex of yours in this generation. You are the devil's gateway. You destroy God's image in man."

The Wind from the East

There is a harsh grandeur about the desert and its implacable indifference to human invasion which seems to have influenced the social customs of the men who dwell there. In the slight traces that remain to us of pre-Islamic Arabian paganism, we find the same alternation between passionate sensualism and drastic asceticism, the same contempt for women as the essential agents of man's pleasure, necessary to him, yet often his undoing, that we find among their medieval successors.

Concubinage, enforced marriage for dynastic purposes, and enslavement by capture, Mahomet found in the society of his youth; and there is evidence that he found also asceticism vowed to total abstinence and celibacy. It is recorded of him that he forbade infanticide—a common expedient among desert peoples confronted habitually by the threat of famine, and confined usually, though not always, to female children. He permitted for the first time women to inherit property, at the rate of fifty per cent. of a man's inheritance. It is not known how far he condoned with the practice of seclusion in the harem. He himself

23

was forced by personal affection to show indulgence towards the adultery of his favourite wife Ayesha, whom scandal could not alienate from his affection, and his private conduct may have alleviated for a few individuals the severity of contemporary judgment.

These were faint relaxations of a grim social code; but the wind from the east blew little good to women. From farther Asia, the Aryan Hindus had passed through a period of comparative freedom and equality not unlike that of the Homeric Greeks; but when with increased homogeneity and political assurance, social customs grew more stable, the purdah and the veil, originally designed as a protection, became a prison. Widow-burning, not mentioned, unless the text is unjustifiably twisted, in the Vedas, and probably adopted from the primitive Dravidians whom the Aryans supplanted, became the common practice in medieval India. It was not peculiar to that country; there are traces of it in Icelandic, Slavonic and German legends; Evadne, wife of one of the "Seven Against Thebes" burned with her husband; four wives were slaughtered and embalmed with Amen-hetep II of Egypt, and the custom can be traced among Fijians, Maoris, Tongans and Africans; but in India it became identified with the Hindu religion and survived until within living memory. Even to-day the doctrines which, carried to their logical conclusion, led widows to the funeral pyre, still lay the responsibility for the husband's salvation upon his wife, still condemn widows to expiate in prayer, fasting and self-sacrifice their husband's death, still enforce the Alcestic ideal upon Hindu girls.

However much the West might consider itself detached from the East, the harem, the purdah, the veil and the sati, with all their psychological implications, have exercised a constantly recurring influence upon the position of women throughout the world.

The Church and the Barbarians

Polemists attacking Christianity have tried to prove that
its influence after the first century A.D. was wholly baleful
to women, quoting the Pauline doctrine of female subservience, quoting the explosions of anger by the Early
Fathers against women as temptresses of men's frail flesh,
quoting the exclusion of women from the Catholic priest-
hood, the exaggerated importance of celibacy, the social
conditions which survived the decline of the Roman
Empire and the Dark Ages in Europe.

It is perfectly true that as canon law developed, it
stiffened by legal sanction a relationship in which women
were in every way placed at the mercy of husbands, fathers
and other male relatives; but this subordination was more
Roman than Christian. The Catholic Church inherited
more than an earthly habitation from the city of St. Peter.
The canon law conclusions concerning women were based
upon the foundation of the *Patria Potestas*. Saul of Tarsus
inherited two traditions—the Eastern suspicion of women
as the delight and seduction of masculine frailty, and the
Roman legal axiom of paternal authority. It was unfortunate that the liberality of the Christian vision was not
powerful enough to destroy these deeply-rooted influences.

Yet canon law did modify the severity of Roman practice as it modified the ferocity of Oriental prejudice. By
teaching that women had immortal souls, it set a limit upon
the morality of coercion. Wives must submit themselves
to their husbands—even if this meant death by excessive
and dangerous child-bearing, if it meant the sacrifice of
friends, relatives, children, property; fathers were the sole
guardians of their legitimate children and might control
completely all their actions; but at least there was a limit
to what husbands and fathers might righteously command.
The Church tried to check paternal despotism not by
decreasing its legal powers but by preaching mercy to

fathers. It tried to protect the rights of wives by raising the marriageable age of girls to twelve and by discouraging physical cruelty. By idealising the Virgin Mary it softened the brutality of a code ready enough to regard women wholly as instruments for pleasure or breeding.

At the same time it is true that the Puritan doctrines of extreme asceticism did harm to women by emphasising their sexual function beyond all other human qualities and by associating it, and therefore them, with sin. The resulting fear and prejudice set a great gulf between men and women which could not easily be bridged and which still too often poisons their relationship.

Yet the fruits of asceticism were not wholly harmful. If Puritanism endangered natural love and mutual respect, the monastic system which also gained emotional validity from the ideal of self-sacrifice for the glory of God, brought certain definite advantages in its train.

The idea of celibate men and women living in dedicated communities is older and wider than Christianity. Egypt and Babylon had their temple priestesses, Rome her vestal virgins; Buddhism was to be served by bands of vagrant almswomen; Islam by its Sufi mystics. In periods when women were apt to be regarded as instruments of pleasure, labour-chattels, and breeding-stock, without dignity, humanity, or integrity of personality, it was of immense significance that contemporary thought could recognise and respect their individual religious vocation. If it was not without importance that Mary of Nazareth should be worshipped as the Mother of God, neither was it unimportant that women such as Catherine of Siena or Theresa of Spain or, indeed, the Islamic mystic, Rabia of Basra, should be recognised as spiritual leaders and divinely inspired saints. In monotheistic religions, unlike polytheistic paganism, God was described as masculine and His chosen prophets or incarnations were men; but women could rise to a high comprehension of divinity and by their spiritual prestige regain some of the dignity of which tradition had deprived their sex.

Nor was this the sole advantage of the monastic law. It has been most commonly praised for the shelter it provided to women during the violence and insecurity of the Dark Ages. But masculine historians have frequently tended to over-estimate the desirability of protection for women. Far more important, convents and nunneries provided scope for the exercise of certain faculties which might otherwise have atrophied. Learning and the arts could be practised in the more liberal orders. The high craft of administration was requisite everywhere. Abbess Hilda of Whitby ruled a community of men as well as of women, and made her northern Abbey a centre of religious and cultural life. Hrotsvita of Gaudersheim in Saxony not only collected a famous library but was herself a dramatist of authentic if limited power. It was to a convent that Christina de Pisan, author of the *Feats and Arms of Chivalry* printed by Caxton, perhaps the first successful woman journalist, retired towards the end of her stormy life.

Education, the practice of organised social welfare, the care of the poor, the treatment of the sick, the control of estates and farms, responsibility for funds, the handling of large, varied and often widely scattered communities— all these activities demand virtues of intellect and character impossible to associate with the acquiescent domestic chattel approved by Roman Law. The convent provided opportunities for their exercise—a decisive and important step towards women's emancipation—but a side-step. Underlying the modern controversy about the right of married women to earn, and the entire problem of women's education and employment, remains the feeling inherited from conventual tradition that women employed in non-domestic occupations should be celibate. The convent gave women their chance at a price which they are still paying—the separation of the idea of intellectual and

27

administrative activity from the idea of normal biological fulfilment.

Both classes of women suffered and still suffer from this separation. From the Dark Ages onwards, the average married woman has lived largely deprived of opportunities for satisfying her natural instincts of intellectual curiosity and impersonal enthusiasm, while the few women enjoying these latter satisfactions have commonly been confronted by a demand to abandon the prospect of motherhood—alternatives which have proved wholesome neither to domestic nor to non-domestic achievement.

But that is not the whole story. It may have been in various ways unfortunate that the Church was the main guardian of culture in the period following the collapse of the Roman Empire; but the fact remains that it did prove a guardian. It kept alive in scattered centres throughout the Dark Ages the lights of learning, impersonal enthusiasm for truth and beauty, and values not wholly dominated by material standards, which might otherwise have vanished utterly from a distracted world. And because the complete humanity of women can adequately be fulfilled only under civilised conditions, this preservation was important.

The customs of the barbarian invaders themselves were not unfavourable to women. The Scandinavian rovers and the Germanic tribes both shared the dignity and freedom of the Homeric age. The parasitism of the Roman lady was as foreign to them as the seclusion of the Indian purdah. But the turmoil of the invasions and the social insecurity resulting from them, affected the very women who might otherwise have been reassured by the spiritual liberalism of Christianity or invigorated by the rude liberties of barbarism.

An age of upheaval becomes dominated by military values. The feudal system, evolved to meet the needs of a troubled time, was founded upon war service and land holding. Medieval war service, though not impossible to women, found them at a disadvantage because of their lighter build and smaller muscular power; landholding was made largely dependent upon war service. Daughters might have dowries, and marriage became part of the complex dynastic game for land acquisition; but girls were in subjection to their fathers, if they were free, and to their lords if they were villeins. Landlords practised the *jus primæ noctis* upon the virgin daughters of their tenants as part of their legal privilege; fathers, if policy dictated, betrothed babies, and married them off while still helpless children to men old enough to be their grandfathers. Husbands got their wives with children as early and as often as they chose and could, and between legal insecurity and the natural handicap of frequent pregnancy, women had little opportunity even for the rebellious thought which inspires protest. It was right at the end of the Middle Ages that Erasmus put into the mouth of a bride words as applicable to the eighteenth-century squire's wife as to the pawns of medieval ambition: "What a hell is marriage! What a slave's business! And for whom, ye gods. For a gambler, a brute, a rake! 'Twould be far better to sleep with a pig."

On the other hand, the social and economic life of feudal Europe at least provided adequate occupation for all but court retainers. The vacuous misery of ladyhood did not afflict women to whom was committed the domestic care of inconvenient castles, each more a combination of barracks, hospital, hotel and boarding-school, than a family residence. All forms of home industry were practised, and if the nobleman's wife did not herself spin, weave, brew, bake, distill herb medicines, cure skins, dye clothes and repair armour, she frequently had the task of supervising these necessities. The poorer women in the town-shared their husbands' craft or followed their own as spinsters, lace-makers, helmet-makers and the like; they belonged to guilds; they had their pride of workmanship;

29

in the country dairies, stock breeding, and almost all forms of agricultural labour except—as a rule—ploughing and threshing, were women's work as much as men's. So the bitterest wrong of wasted energy and stifled vigour was not done to women. If life was hard, personal relationships crude and the law unfavourable, at least the day's work had to be done, and it was worth doing.

The Age of Chivalry

Into this singularly unsentimental world of necessity and interest the first romantic movement introduced a new conception of woman's place. As Western Europe settled down after the incursions and destructions of the Dark Ages, the rigidity of military vigilance relaxed. Society grew gentler; security bred leisure; leisure gave opportunity for a recurrence of interest not only in the arts of learning, but in modes and manners and personality. The fashions for courtesy and chivalry, the idealisation of romantic love, the renewed emphasis upon personal affections, affected women's position in ways both good and bad.

It was good that troubadours and pages and men-about-court should idealise certain women; that beauties such as Eleanor of Aquitaine should be saluted at tournaments, and that manners should lose a little of their brutality. It was bad that respect for women should be associated, not with ability or achievement, but with pride of birth or youth or physical beauty. When courtesy was identified with chivalry, and chivalry with protection, the result was not to open opportunities for women, but to close them. Ultimately few European fashions have done more harm to women than the romanticism which celebrated their natures as divine and a glance from their eyes as adequate reward for masculine endeavour.

There were women who realised the fraud. That shrewd widow, Christine de Pisan, in a story from her *Le Livre des*

Trois Vertus, counsels one heroine of such adoration to set aside idle thoughts and do a little useful work instead. Joanna of Naples, one of the most spectacular "queens of love," had moments when she preferred the enduring pleasures of learning to the rather ambiguous position of a court beauty. There were women who tolerated chivalry as a useful convenience, and exercised real power, administering estates for husbands absent years together, fighting or controlling scattered manors. There were women who broke straight through conventions and insisted upon the full exercise of their powers—such as the half-legendary Belissia Gotzadina of Bologna, who became a doctor of civil and common law when she was twenty-seven, and one of the most popular lecturers in the university.

But these were the exceptions. For the most part women accepted the place in society indicated by their disabilities for war-service—the foundation upon which the entire organisation rested. Further east, in Russia, in the Balkans, and wherever the influence of the Mahometan invasions had passed, things were far worse for them. The Orthodox Greek church was less liberal in its attitude than the Catholic; Islam was deliberately hostile. "I have not left any calamity more hurtful to man than women," Mahomet once declared, sharing Tertullian's opinion. Doughty's observations in *Arabia Deserta* might equally have been true of the contemporaries of St. Joan. "The woman's lot is here unequal concubinage and in this necessitous life a weary servitude. The possession in her of parents has been yielded at some price to a husband, by whom she may be dismissed in what day he shall have no more pleasure in her." Christian marriage at least gave the wife security, even if it were the security of the chattel.

"A hen is not a bird nor a woman a human being," runs the old Russian proverb. The medieval Russian terem was a kind of harem. The Domstroy, a domestic ordinance drawn up in the sixteenth century, advised a husband to

31

beat his wife if she disobeyed him, "but not in the presence of others, rather alone . . . and do not strike her in the face or on the ear. . . . For he who allows himself to be carried away to such actions in anger may have much unpleasantness, if for instance she loses her hearing or goes blind or breaks a bone in her hand or foot or elsewhere." The *jus primæ noctis*, which disappeared in England with the end of the feudal system, endured in France and Germany on certain estates until the eighteenth century, in Russia, until the 1917 revolution.

The Renaissance and the Puritan

The stage in European civilisation which we call the Renaissance had, like the fashion of chivalry, a double effect upon women's position. Individual women gained new opportunities for intellectual and artistic development. There were the daughters of Sir Thomas More in Chelsea, Vittoria Colonna and Beatrice d'Este in Italy, Marguerite of Navarre at Paris, Lady Jane Grey and Elizabeth Tudor—these women had not only trained intellects and well-developed æsthetic taste—they had spirit and pride and authority. When Shakespeare drew his portraits of Rosalind, Portia, Beatrice, and Desdemona, he clearly lived in a world where, however harshly the law might discriminate against women and custom curb their action, they yet lived as free creatures with unrepressed vitality self-confidence and wit. The natural resilience of the human creature, aided by a more civilised standard of life, had overcome, as it had recurrently throughout the past, the disabilities of tradition.

Social life was changing. The manor-house had replaced the castle; comfort supplanted grandeur. Villeinage in England (not till much later across the Channel), was abolished, though peasants grew poorer and became a landless proletariat as the commons were enclosed. A middle class was arising and substituting for gentility of birth a gentility of wealth. Domesticity increased, habits became more humane, and manners more gentle, as houses became more comfortable. Life for well-to-do women grew easier; for the poor, it changed little throughout the centuries until the Industrial Revolution.

In Protestant countries the individualism of the reformed religion provided a foundation upon which the later protests of feminist rebels were to be based; if what mattered most was neither community nor tradition but the individual soul before its Maker, then women as well as men had souls to save and integrity of conviction to preserve. So far so good.

But with Protestantism came puritanism, and its revival of the ascetic tradition and the distrust of the body. Because men could derive pleasure from women's bodies, and pleasure was sin, therefore women themselves were instruments of evil. The old pagan instinct of revulsion from uncleanliness stirred again in the Institutes of Calvin and the sermons and pamphlets of John Knox. While social prejudice and organisation confined women to those activities most closely associated with their biological functions—to the breeding and rearing of children, and the charming and cherishing of husbands—Puritan philosophy taught them to associate those biological functions with something sinister and undesirable.

So self-contradictory and unnatural a philosophy of life could not for long dictate a social system; but it has for centuries coloured the attitude towards sex and maternity, not in Protestant countries alone. It actively affects the position of women in the world to-day. We call it Puritanism, but we forget that before it was Protestant it was Catholic, before it was Christian it was Hebrew; before it was Hebrew it was pagan. It runs back into the early roots of human history, when women were creatures enduring inexplicable physical experiences, whose bodies exuded magic that might rob the mightiest hunter of virility.

Protestantism did another disservice to women. By the abolition of the monasteries it deprived them of the one type of institution where they had learned the craft of administration and played the political game. Secular schools replaced the education of the convent; and during the seventeenth century girls' boarding-schools sprang up all over England. Bathsua Malkin's famous establishment at Tottenham High Cross boasted a formidable curriculum, to which was added this significant rider: "Those that think one language enough for a woman may forbear the languages and learn only experimental philosophy." But however experimental the philosophy, the fact remained that unmarried women were now deprived of the only institution which valued their personalities as highly as that of the wives and mothers; "old maids" were now bidden to lead their apes in hell. The conventual system may have been a blind alley; but at least it offered an alley—a place of withdrawal and privilege which had its unquestionable uses.

Three Revolutions

The common sense and rationalism of eighteenth-century Western Europe weakened the influence of Puritanism, or rather, drove it downward through society to re-emerge among the pietists of the Evangelical movement, and to be bequeathed by them, strengthened and elaborated, to the epoch that we call Victorian.

But during the eighteenth century three movements of immense importance undoubtedly did radically affect the position of women, not only in this country but in Western Europe and later throughout the world. The first was the evolution of the leisured lady; the second the Industrial Revolution; the third, the French Revolution. Of the three, the evolution of the leisured lady has had probably the most persistent, as well as the most pernicious, consequences.

There had of course been ladies before the eighteenth century; but when society was less flexible, before the rise of capitalism provided a great solvent of social customs, when manners were rough and domestic architecture uncomfortable, the peculiar quality of ladyhood could seldom exist and still more seldom exercise any influence outside its own sphere. Mrs. Pepys might sometimes dress to look like Lady Castlemaine, but she rose at three o'clock in the morning to do the household washing, and though, being childless, she sometimes found time hang heavy on her hands and even occasionally stayed in bed till eight in the morning "for mirth," she had small opportunity to feel that wretchedness of futility against which Mary Wollstonecraft, Florence Nightingale and a hundred others were later to protest.

The eighteenth-century lady was the product of a combination of circumstances. In both France and England, at the end of the seventeenth century, society was stabilised, and stability led to a refinement of manners, growth of domestic comfort, extension of secular education and the establishment of a more sociable urban life. In this country the growth of the wool trade, imperial expansion, land enclosures, and the victory, in the political contests of the past hundred years, of the middle classes, had created a new type of prosperous citizen who liked to display his wife and daughters as symbols of his success, for another tenet of Puritanism affecting English morality was the association of prosperity with righteousness.

The new domestic architecture facilitated social gatherings impossible in the days of flaring torches and huge ill-lighted halls. In France, the refinements of the Rambouillet Salon, in England the urbanities of Berkeley Square, won for society at large a new standard of civilised intercourse, at the cost of displaying a most unfortunate model for women to copy. It was not the learning of Lady Mary Wortley Montagu nor the wit of Madame du

Deffand which could be widely imitated, but the fact that
ladies did no work but "fancy" work, that they undertook
no responsibility beyond the organisation of a household
and the care of a family, and that these, if they were rich
enough, they delegated to paid employees; that they passed
their time in conversation, card-playing, dancing and the
pursuit of elegance; that even their children were removed
as quickly as possible to the care of wet-nurses, governesses,
and mistresses of boarding-schools. The greater the leisure,
the more complete the lady. She was the first waste
product of the new economic system, the most elaborate
extravagance of conspicuous consumption.

During the reign of Queen Anne a little satire called
The Town Ladies' Catechism mocked this social ideal:

"How do you employ your time now?" asks the
questioner.

The lady replies: "I lie in bed till noon, dress all afternoon, dine in the evening and play cards till midnight."

"How do you spend the Sabbath?"

"In chit-chat."

"What do you talk of?"

"New fashions and new plays."

"Pray, Madame, what books do you read?"

"I read lewd plays and winning romances."

"Who is it you love?"

"My self."

"What, nobody else?"

"My page, my monkey and my lap-dog."

Satire is not to be taken as serious evidence. It is true
that there were pious ladies, philanthropic ladies, learned
ladies, maternal ladies, ladies with political interests, as
well as card-players and scandal-mongers; but individual
virtues do not redeem a pernicious system. During the
eighteenth century the idleness of female members of a
family became the sign of its gentility. Few worse evils
have ever happened to women.

The Industrial Revolution being itself a complex movement had a complex effect upon women's position. The mechanisation of industry, the factory system, and the growth of cities, by enriching the middle class facilitated the diffusion of the leisured lady ideal. The increase of population which followed, and the cult of the large family, profoundly affected domestic life; and the industrialisation of the poorer classes brought into mines, factories and workshops, women and girls of every size and age who were not rich enough to escape them.

Women did not originally choose to enter industry; they were driven in as an alternative to starvation for themselves and for their families. That is perhaps one of the reasons why so many authorities to-day think that women should not be allowed to leave industry and the professions of their own accord; they should be driven out. The enclosure system had first forced peasants out of agriculture into home industries—chain-making, weaving, spinning, or carpentry; the use of machinery forced them out of home industry. They could not compete with the machines; they must serve them, and to serve them they must move into the squalid new settlements spreading round the factories, mines and mills. They must leave their homes and work for twelve hours a day or longer under a master's roof; they must leave small children to the care of a neighbour, or bring them to work as soon as they could; they must neglect the houses that had been their responsibility, forget the domestic crafts which had been their pride, and subordinate all personal affection to the economic pressure of the times.

Consequently, the idea of women's work outside the home in industry became associated with squalor, fatigue, bad cooking and neglected children, just as the idea of women's work in the professions became associated with celibacy, aggressiveness or impropriety, and with everything contradictory to the ideal of ladyhood. In addition, the increasing mass-production of articles formerly made in the home reduced one by one the former duties of the housewife. While fashion dictated idleness to the well-to-do the new industrial system made it possible. The cleavage between the overworked factory woman and the underworked lady widened; both suffered.

But they had one bond in common. Both, under the law, were in a state of servitude. The property alike of heiress-bride or half-stripped nail-maker belonged not to her but to her husband. Her earnings were his as well as her inherited estate. Women themselves belonged as a sometimes embarrassing property to fathers or to husbands. They were not the legal guardians of their own legitimate children nor the proprietors of their own persons. "By marriage," said Blackstone in his great *Commentaries on the laws of England*, "the very being or legal existence of woman is suspended, or at least it is incorporated and consolidated into that of the husband, under whose wing protection and cover she performs everything, and she is therefore called in our law a femme-couvert." "Couvert" she might be. The right of husbands to imprison wives in their own houses did not end till 1891.

All property belonged to the husband, not to the wife. The home was his. He could do what he liked with it. The children were his. He could send them into boarding-schools, take them to foreign countries, place them under guardians, choose their tutors, religious teaching and companions. Husbands had full rights over their wives' persons. Protest was immoral, and at a time when scientific means of birth control were practically unknown among respectable families, this meant that husbands could, if they chose, keep their wives bound upon a perpetually turning wheel of pregnancy and childbirth, till their age or death released them. And there was no escape. Before 1857 no woman could obtain a divorce except after an immensely complicated business through Act of Parliament. In the whole history of England, only two women achieved this. It was not wonderful that in such circumstances husband-murder was, until 1784, legally termed "petty treason" and punishable by burning.

But not many wives attempted this or any less drastic method of escape. In every age and among both sexes rebels are rarer than conformists. The Hitler election of November, 1933, in Germany showed what unanimity of acquiescence can be secured in a civilised and highly educated country once the recognised leaders of an opposition have been removed. In pre-revolutionary England, there were few leaders among women to remove, and these had their good reasons for conformity. There had been the educationalists, Hannah Woolley, Mary Astell, Elizabeth Elston; there had been the blue stockings, Fanny Burney, Mrs. Thrale, and Hannah More; but these were not all rebels. It is true that the Sunday School movement initiated by the virtuous Miss More and Mrs. Linmer had far-reaching social consequences; but its founders would have been the first to deplore these. Hannah More detested Mary Wollstonecraft, and declared she could see nothing in her educational works except seduction, nor in her claim for the Rights of Women more than a justification of adultery. Like many good women she had learned to believe in her own virtues, and in the circumstances amid which they were cultivated. "Girls should be led to distrust their own judgment," she declared. "They should learn not to murmur at expostulation; they should be accustomed to expect and to endure opposition. It is a lesson with which the world will not fail to furnish them; and they will not practise it the worse for having learned it the sooner. It is of the last importance to their happiness, even in this life, that they should acquire a submissive temper and a forbearing spirit. They must even endure to be thought wrong sometimes, when they cannot but feel they are right."

Submission, sensibility, solicitude—these were the qualities marking the virtuous woman, in eighteenth-century London as in third-century Athens, B.C.

It was into this society that at the close of the century, were hurled the doctrines of liberty, equality and fraternity. Not, of course that society as a whole chose at once to listen. The ladies of Bath and Belgravia no more welcomed the tenets of Jacobinism after the fall of the Bastille than they welcomed the tenets of Bolshevism after the capture of the Kremlin. But the French Revolution shook established ideas far more profoundly than it unsettled established orders. In 1792 Mary Wollstonecraft published her *Vindication of the Rights of Women.*

CHAPTER II

THE VINDICATION OF HUMANITY

The Importance of Mary Wollstonecraft

THE importance of Mary Wollstonecraft lies in her genius for indiscretion during an age when a woman's first duty was to be discreet. So far as her *Vindication of the Rights of Women* is concerned, it is a bad book, straggling, grandiloquent, uneven; it violated contemporary sentiment, was condemned by contemporary judgment, and sank into temporary oblivion after the premature death of its writer. Yet it is a great book; great in its vision, its passion, its independence. After a brief period of neglect, its message suddenly appeared relevant to the nineteenth century. It has been reprinted eighteen times, its latest edition dated 1929, and it has become the bible of the women's movement in Great Britain.

Mary Wollstonecraft's predecessors, Mary Astell, Catherine Macaulay and Condorcet, whose essay *Sur l'admission des femmes au droit de cité* she much admired, attacked educational or political disabilities of women. Mary Wollstonecraft went to the heart of the matter: "The first object of laudable ambition is to obtain a character as a human being, regardless of the distinction of sex, and . . . secondary views should be brought to this simple touchstone." So she launched her courage, her intelligence, and her anger, against the restriction of women's education, the curtailment of their civil and political rights, and the subjugation of their persons, and she dedicated her protest to Talleyrand, the bland agile sophisticated diplomat who had once written: "that to see one half of the human race excluded by the other from all participation of government was a political phenomenon that, according to abstract principles, it was impossible to explain." Reckless in her affections as in her opinions, she outraged what was perhaps the strongest passion among women of her age—the passion for propriety; but it was precisely that outrage which impressed her personality and her revolt upon her age. A woman who had, as a child, defied her father, as a girl defied her brother-in-law, as a woman originated a new educational technique, travelled to revolutionary France in admiration of its political experiment, taken a lover and borne a child to him, travelled alone on business in Norway, attempted suicide, lived with her legal husband before marrying him, and published books as bold in their argument as they were impassioned in their style, was unlikely to live unobserved in eighteenth-century England.

Her rebellion had something of the liberating effect of the militant suffrage movement which, over a hundred years later, was again to violate that sentiment of propriety which has always been one of the chief obstacles to women's independence. Educated to please, to attract, to console, a woman inevitably found opposition to current standards of value difficult. It demanded of her an almost monstrous repudiation of what she had always been told should be her nature. Nothing short of a psychological revolution was needed to achieve that change for which Mary Wollstonecraft laboured—"to obtain a character as a human being."

A century and a half has passed since she returned to England after her tragic visit to Portugal to see her friend and colleague, Fanny Blood, die in childbirth. During that time the position of women in the civilised world has changed in almost every particular. Its curious contradictions and anomalies to-day are largely due to the clash between Mary Wollstonecraft's ideal of humanity, and the sub-human functional ideas of its opponents before and after her.

The Vindication of Citizenship

The movement towards the political emancipation of women in Western Europe arose directly from the ideas circulating at the time of the French Revolution. Directly, but not immediately.

The "dawn" in which it was bliss to be alive and very heaven to be young revealed itself only to a small minority. Mary Wollstonecraft, the young Wordsworth, Shelley, Godwin and Thomas Paine were exceptional, not characteristic. But the public is influenced even by what it dislikes, and ideas from across the Channel affected the position of English women in unexpected ways.

The new humanitarianism of the romantic movement, by encouraging sensibility and preaching individualism, was partly responsible for the beginning of improvement in women's legal position. By 1817 the public whipping of women delinquents had been abandoned; Elizabeth Fry's penal reform, reminding people of the essential humanity even of female criminals, helped to prepare a psychological background for women's legal recognition. In 1836 the case of the Hon. Caroline Norton called attention to the complete impotence before the law of a married woman. When her worthless husband carried off her children and sued Lord Melbourne for "criminal conversation" with his wife, Mrs. Norton found that under the law she had no individual existence. As a married woman she could neither sue nor be sued; she could not be represented by counsel at the trial; she had no rights of guardianship over her children. When, after his desertion, she tried to support herself, her earnings belonged legally to her husband. Because she had been a reigning toast, a fashionable London hostess, a wit and a beauty, her plight

43

received attention denied to less conspicuous sufferers, and her vehement pamphlet, *The Natural Claim of a Mother to the Custody of her Children*, was read and hotly debated; but it was not until the Infants Custody Act of 1925 that married women became the legal guardians of their legitimate children.

In 1855 a well-to-do young amateur, Barbara Leigh Smith, published a *Brief Summary in Plain Language of the Most Important Laws concerning Women*, and a public meeting was called to discuss the property rights of married women; from thenceforward women protested against the disabilities of wives until between the years 1870 and 1908 a series of Married Women's Property Acts transformed their legal position.

The same sense of individual rights led to the demand for reform of the marriage and divorce laws, but when the Matrimonial Causes Act of 1857 was passed it established the principle that though a husband could divorce a wife for adultery alone, she could only divorce him if to adultery he added cruelty, desertion or other crimes. It was not until 1923 that men and women could plead equal grounds for divorce—equal, though inadequate.

A few minor anomalies remain—the inequality of the nationality laws between wives and husbands and the insecurity of the married woman wage-earner; but the whole legal position of women in this country has been revolutionised.

At the beginning of the nineteenth century, every woman was legally only the adjunct of some man—father, guardian or husband. "My wife and I are one and I am he." She had no choice; she had no legal personality; her status was ancillary, dependent upon the will, good or bad, of others. To-day she has the right of contracting into her chosen state. "The movement of the progressive societies has been uniform in one respect," wrote Sir Henry Maine in his *Ancient Law*. "Through all its course it has been distinguished by the gradual dissolution of family dependency and the growth of individual obligation in its place. . . . Thus the status of the slave has disappeared. . . . The status of the female under tutelage. . . . We may say that the movement of progressive societies has hitherto been a movement from status to contract." It remained for the great American judge, Mr Justice Oliver Wendel Holmes to go further and state: "There can be no freedom of contract where there is not equality of status."

A citizen, however, is a person with more than private rights. He has political rights and duties. Talleyrand and Condorcet had recommended the participation by women in the work of government; but that great Whig, Charles James Fox, merely found the notion funny.

In spite of Mary Wollstonecraft's writings, and the Honourable Caroline Norton's appeal for legal justice, the first women to demand political influence were neither intellectuals nor society ladies; they were the industrial workers. Oppressed by the intolerable conditions following the Industrial Revolution, maddened by the hunger of children, the squalor of the disease-breeding warrens into which the new factory-hands were crowded, and the ferocity of the laws which condemned to transportation or the hulks workers convicted of "unlawful assembly," they were driven into protest. When William Cobbett, in 1816, reduced the price of his Radical journal *The Political Register* to twopence, women read it—probably the very women who had been taught their A B C at charity schools intended for the production of docile domestic servants, or at Sunday Schools inspired by Hannah More. Women attended the little insurgent groups meeting in cottages and rick-yards. In 1818 the Radical weaver, Samuel Bamford, whose wife had been his loyal colleague, carried a resolution at Saddlegate that women should be qualified to vote at Radical meetings. A Female Reform Society

45

was established among the cotton spinners of Blackburn. In Sheffield, a Female Political Association sprang up which did not dissolve till 1851. When Castlereagh introduced the Seditious Meetings Bill into parliament in 1819, he thanked God that no women took part in public meetings in the metropolis, and "trusted" that "such a drama would be put an end to by the innate decorum and innate sense of modesty which the women of the country possessed."

Decorum and modesty fought hard. To defy them meant anguish. But from three directions the old prejudices were being assaulted. The working women, their activities driven underground like those of the working men, continued to attend meetings; they were Luddites; they were Chartists. More respectably they became Co-operators. In 1825 the Co-operator, Thompson, published an *Appeal of One Half the Human Race, Women, against the Pretensions of the Other Half, Man.* His collaborator was Mrs. Wheeler, and he stressed the importance of women in the co-operative movement.

Meanwhile the philanthropists were breaking tabus— Elizabeth Fry, Sarah Martin, Louisa Twining who won the right of women to be appointed poor-law guardians, Mary Carpenter who opened the first Ragged School Florence Nightingale and Josephine Butler, proved to men, and, still more significantly, to women, that both sexes had something to contribute to human welfare. They had advantages. Charity was respectable—to do good to the poor a fashionable and even praiseworthy occupation. But it had unforeseen results. In 1846 when the great world Anti-Slavery Convention was held in London, four women arrived among the American delegates. The Convention was outraged, the innovation declared to be "subversive of the principles and tradition of the country and contrary to the word of God." The women were kept shut away in a little gallery behind curtains; but when

46

they went home, they summoned the first Women's Rights Convention at Seneca Falls in 1848.

Direct claims to political enfranchisement were still to be made.

In 1831 the *Westminster Review* published an article by an unknown woman inspired by Benthamism and advocating the then audacious suggestion of female suffrage. The following year Mr. Hunt, M.P., presented to parliament a petition from a wealthy Yorkshire spinster, Mary Smith, of Stanmore, asking "that every unmarried female possessing the necessary pecuniary qualifications should be allowed to vote." In the 1850's a group of active and well-educated young women, whose thoughts were directed towards political enfranchisement through the realisation of their impotence without it to secure social reform, gathered round Barbara Leigh Smith at Langham Place, and began a series of activities which had the most far-reaching effects.

In 1856 John Stuart Mill stood as parliamentary candidate for Westminster, and placed women's suffrage in the forefront of his programme. The group from Langham Place assisted him. Barbara Leigh Smith (now Madame Bodichon) with Emily Davies, the founder of Girton College, actually drove through London in a carriage hung with placards advertising his candidature; women canvassed for him; ladies, who had already been encouraged to hold drawing-room meetings by the Anti-Corn Law League, now began to discuss at these Mill's revolutionary proposal. In 1865 he was elected, and presented to parliament a petition organised by Barbara Bodichon's Women's Suffrage Committee. In May, 1867, when parliamentary reform was being debated, Mill moved an amendment extending the franchise to cover women, and eighty members actually voted for it.

After that, for over sixty years, the matter became a major political issue. Once parliament had seriously discussed the subject, even innate decorum and modesty could not wholly close it again to women. A London Society for Obtaining Political Rights for Women formed committees at Manchester, Edinburgh, Birmingham and Bristol. In 1868 the case of Chorlton *v.* Lings, brought before the Court of Common Pleas, argued the right of women to vote. The judge decided that "every woman is personally incapable." Nothing but a change in the law could do it. The pleader of the women's case was a Dr. Pankhurst.

The issue was now a live one; but the difficulties of working for it were enormous. In 1869 the first public suffrage meeting with a woman, Mrs. Peter Taylor, in the chair, was held in London. It was greeted with ridicule; public speaking by women was derided not only as ridiculous but as immoral. But the women went on. They held meetings in the constituencies. The indefatigable Lydia Becker of Manchester organised the Midlands. In 1870 a suffrage bill drafted by Dr. Pankhurst and introduced by Jacob Bright was quashed in committee by Mr. Gladstone, and with it all hopes of parliamentary victory for many years.

But though the main fortress did not yield, women were gaining access to subsidiary positions. In 1869, almost without a dissentient word, the municipal franchise was extended to women rate-payers; in 1870 Mr. Forster's Education Act enabled them to vote and sit on school boards; five years later Miss Marrington was elected a poor-law guardian. In 1873 Mrs. Nassau Senior became a poor-law inspector, and in 1888 when the county councils came into existence, Lady Sandhurst and Miss Cobden were elected on to the L.C.C. and Miss Cons actually made an Alderman, though, until the Qualification of Women Act, in 1907, women were unable to take their seats.

This was something; but to have the administration of the laws, without responsibility for making them, emphasised the imperfections of the franchise position, and drove intelligent women to concentrate their efforts upon winning the parliamentary vote.

This became even more true after the Reform Bill of 1884, when working men were enfranchised, but women again completely omitted. The suffrage societies were growing, and suffering from the inconveniences of growth. In 1871 they were split by the controversy surrounding Josephine Butler's campaign against the Contagious Diseases Act; after 1884, the Primrose League and Women's Liberal Federation distracted the attention of many women to purely party political issues. By 1889 the suffrage movement was sufficiently influential to win the compliment of direct opposition. A solemn protest against it was signed by Mrs. Humphry Ward, Mrs. Crichton and Mrs. Sidney Webb (then Beatrice Potter). In 1892 and 1897 new suffrage bills were unsuccessfully introduced at Westminster; but between those dates first New Zealand then South Australia enfranchised women, and the South African War, justified in England by the Uitlander's cry of "No taxation without representation," reinforced the constitutional argument for women's suffrage.

But though the movement grew in size and self-confidence, the great mass of people were unconcerned and unstirred. Approval was for the most part academic; the opposition alone impassioned. "What use would the vote be to me?" the average woman asked sceptically. In 1903 a new phenomenon arose. A group of women who had been working among the factory hands in Manchester led by Mrs. Pankhurst, founded the Women's Social and Political Union. When in 1904 Mr. Begg's Franchise Bill was "talked out" of the debate, they lost patience. Other revolts had succeeded only after unconstitutional methods. Mr. Gladstone, regarded as arch-enemy of women's franchise, had himself declared: "I am sorry to say that if no instructions had been addressed in political crises to the people of this country except to remember to hate violence, to love order and to exercise patience, the liberties of this country would never have been attained."

Women were naturally disposed to hate violence and love order. They had received a centuries-long training in the exercise of patience. All violence violated their biological tendency to preserve rather than to destroy; but the constant betrayal of promises and delay of justice overcame traditional inclination. In 1905 the militant movement began.

It was a movement which stirred England from end to end. It aroused the wildest antipathy and enthusiasm. At first it took the purely passive form of placing women in a position where the law was bound to inflict suffering upon them, and by its harshness, to advertise their cause and their persistence. The Pankhurst family, Emmeline Pankhurst the vivid, heroic, magnetic orator, and her daughters Christobel, Adelaide and Sylvia, threw themselves into the organisation of revolt. Their attack was launched against the Liberal Government which had repeatedly betrayed them. Their cry was "Is your party going to give votes to women?" Their methods were unprecedented both for women and for rebels. For they interrupted meetings, held illegal processions, lobbied members of parliament *en masse* and picketed ministers' houses, until for these technical offences they were imprisoned.

Until 1909 they attempted no active violence; but in 1910 the Government, finding itself ridiculous, issued orders that suffragettes no longer were to be arrested. That did not suit the W.S.P.U. Mrs. Pankhurst and Christobel worked out a technique of brilliantly conceived provocative action. They would not, like the rebels in Ireland, the Russian Anarchists or Italian Carbonari, fight and drill; but they would strike policemen with their hands, they would break windows, and even later as the opposition grew fiercer, the enthusiasm more recklessly determined, set fire to property. It was a unique rebellion, in that no single attempt was made upon the life of an opponent. One woman, Emily Davison, dashing on to the Epsom course on Derby Day tried to stop the King's horse, thus possibly risking the jockey's life. She was killed; the jockey lived to carry a wreath to Mrs. Pankhurst's funeral inscribed: "To do honour to the memory of Mrs. Pankhurst and Miss Emily Davison."

The result of this campaign was tremendous. Within the women's movement, the suffrage societies divided and divided, the militants from the constitutionalists, the democrats from the autocrats. In 1907 the Women's Freedom League under the Pethick Lawrences split from they W.S.P.U. under the Pankhursts. The constitutionalists under Mrs. Millicent Fawcett deplored the methods of both. But it was Mrs. Pankhurst who set the country ablaze. In and out of prison, hunger-striking, starving, evading arrest by strategems that seemed miraculous, she and her followers provided a constant cause of amazement to the public. The political battle went on; the Conciliation Bill of 1911 passed its second reading; in November Mr. Asquith's promises secured a brief truce in militancy; but when in 1912 the Bill was again defeated on a technical point, dishonouring Asquith's own word, hostilities were renewed. "If it had been Mr. Asquith's object to enrage every woman to the point of fury," wrote the imperturbable Mrs. Fawcett, "he could not have acted with greater perspicacity."

The militants were not imperturbable. Between 1912 and August, 1914, their campaign was unceasing. Mr. McKenna's "Cat and Mouse" Act made it possible to release and re-arrest hunger-strikers. Many women were maimed for life by the rigours of forcible feeding. Lady Constance Lytton disguised herself as a poor seamstress to prove the differentiation of treatment between aristocratic and proletarian prisoners. Nurse Ellen Pitfield died of cancer from a wound received in an interrupted procession, leaving as her legacy to women the words: "There are only two things that matter to me in the world: principle and liberty. For these I will fight as long as there is life in my veins. I am no longer an individual; I am an instrument."

The outbreak of war interrupted the campaign. The W.S.P.U. at once called off its activities. But in June, 1917, when after a Speakers' conference on the subject, the House of Commons by a majority of seven to one enfranchised women over thirty, it was not a little the memory of the militants' determination which influenced them. In February, 1918, the Representation of the People Act became law, but the final grant of equal suffrage to men and women alike was not obtained till, after ten years of post-war agitation, the Royal assent was given to the Representation of the People Act in 1928.

Meanwhile under the Parliament (qualification of women) Act, 1918, women could be elected members of the House of Commons, and Viscountess Astor took her seat for the Southern Division of Plymouth in 1919. The first woman Minister of the Crown was Miss Margaret Bondfield, who became Parliamentary Secretary to the Minister of Labour in 1924, and Cabinet Minister in 1929. The Sex Disqualification (Removal) Act of 1919 theoretically provided that no woman should be disqualified by sex or marriage from the exercise of any public function; but actually there has not yet been an English woman ambassador, chief of police or high court judge; peeresses may not yet take their seats with peers in the House of Lords.

The suffrage movement had enfranchised women, and from more than their lack of citizenship. It had disproved those theories about their own nature which were—and still sometimes are—among their gravest handicaps. This was the great value of militancy. It broke down hitherto infrangible tabus. It was no longer after 1905 possible perpetually to convince an intelligent girl that women cared nothing for impersonal issues, since women had been ready to jeopardise their lives for them, and—worse ordeal—to make themselves ridiculous. It was no longer possible to convince her that women were incapable of political acumen, since their leaders had shown powers of strategy and action unsurpassed in struggles for reform. Women had accepted discipline, displayed capacity of organisation, courage and tenacity. The very recklessness and extremism of militancy had shaken old certainties. An emotional earthquake had shattered the intangible yet suffocating prison of decorum. The standard of values which rated women's persons, position, interests and pre-occupations as affairs of minor national importance had been challenged.*

The Vindication of Intelligence

Political emancipation is a condition of freedom; it is not freedom itself. Mary Wollstonecraft had placed educational reform at the forefront of her demands; Florence Nightingale had cried out against intellectual starvation. "To have no food for our heads, no food for our hearts, no food for our activity, is that nothing? If we have no food for the body, how do we cry out, how all the world hears of it, how all the newspapers talk of it, with a paragraph headed in great capital letters, Death from Starvation! But suppose one were to put a paragraph in the *Times*, Death of Thought from Starvation, or, Death of Moral Activity from Starvation, how people would stare, how they would laugh and wonder!" At the beginning of the nineteenth century, except for a few exceptional daughters of unconventional parents, or rebels like Mary Wollstonecraft, women were not educated as human beings; they were not even, as one pioneer headmistress put it, "trained to be wives; only to get husbands." As Sydney Smith explained: "The system of female education

* See Appendix II, p. 198

as it now stands aims only at embellishing a few years of life which are, in themselves, so full of grace and happiness that they hardly want it, and then leaves the rest a prey to idle insignificance."

When the century opened there was no system of national elementary education for girls or boys. There were ragged schools and Sunday schools and village dame schools which some more fortunate working girls attended. Secondary education for girls was left first to governesses then to private schools of varying efficiency, then to the very small body of endowed schools, such as the Red Maids, Bristol; Howell's School, Llandaff; or the Clergy Daughters' School, Casterton, immortalised in *Jane Eyre* by Charlotte Brontê. To all these forms of education the criticism of the Schools Inquiry Commission of 1864 could be justly applied: "The two capital defects of the teachers of girls are these: they have not themselves been taught and they do not know how to teach." Of teachers' training colleges, university education, or higher-grade technical schools for women there were none.

The first step towards reform was characteristic of its age. In 1841 the Governesses' Benevolent Institution was formed to relieve "privately and delicately" ladies in distress. The stories it revealed of genteel starvation constituted an appalling indictment of social conditions; but the prime need was not for charity but for training. In 1848, largely as a result of the revelations made by the Benevolent Institution, Queen's College for Women was opened in London and the following year, Bedford College, "to teach all branches of female knowledge." They were intended to train governesses; they bred pioneers. George Eliot and Barbara Leigh Smith attended Bedford College, Sophia Jex Blake and Octavia Hill went to Queen's. The desire for education spread. In 1850 Miss Buss founded the North London Collegiate School for Girls; eight years later Miss Beale, who had taught, with angry contempt for its scholastic standards, at Casterton, took over Cheltenham College, a school for ladies already decaying after four years' existence. In 1870 the system of national elementary education founded in this country included girls as well as boys. The movement for reform of women's education had started well.

But it suffered from three great disadvantages. The first was lack of steady objective. Were girls to be educated along the same lines as boys—or differently? The second was inferiority of training among women teachers. The third was the insidious pressure of tradition and home influence.

The first disadvantage has been the subject of a long controversy lasting from 1863 to 1923—from the Cambridge experiment in opening temporarily to girls its Local Examinations, to the Hadow Report on "Differentiation of Curricula between the Sexes in Secondary Schools." When examinations were first opened to girls, one headmistress protested that they would "foster the spirit of confidence and independence which is too common among girls of the present day." Even Miss Beale "desired to institute no comparison between the mental abilities of boys and girls" which might unfit the latter for "that subordinate part in the world to which I believe they have been called." But other educationalists felt differently. Emily Davies, the founder of Girton, Miss Lumsden, the founder of St. Leonard's School, Miss Lawrence of Roedean, the Trustees of the Girls' Public Day School Company, instituted in 1872 to give to girls "the best education possible corresponding with the education given to boys in the great public schools," realised that if girls had to earn their living, if they had to take their place in society, if they wished to vindicate their humanity—or even, indeed, if they wished to make satisfactory wives and mothers—their education should approximate to, not differ from, the education offered to their competitors, colleagues, husbands and sons.

Miss Beale, no apostle of equality, declared, "I think it is good for boys and girls to have similar tastes, that their minds may not be entirely bent in different ways, so that in after life they should understand and be interested in the same things." So the first stage of women's education, "the stage of difference based on inequality; the stage of female accomplishments . . . the stage of educational inefficiency" passed into the second, when "the cause of efficiency was identified with that of equality, and, in the name of both, educational reforms claimed and sought to secure, that there should be no differing between the education of girls and that of boys." The wording is that of the Hadow Committee which, in 1923, was instituted to inquire whether the time had come to pass on to a third stage—that of differentiation without inequality, and which found that "our inquiry has not imbued us with any conviction that there are clear and ascertained differences between the two sexes on which an educational policy may readily be based." In fact, education never was identical. Even in co-educational elementary and secondary schools, distinctions arose. Both the evidence given before the Hadow Commission, and the existing state of educational opinion in this country, prove that this first problem of objective has not yet been completely solved. Should education be directed towards emphasising or eliminating the differences that exist between the sexes? In spite of the Hadow Report, opinion still wavers.

The second problem was that of teaching the teachers. It was met by the campaign for entrance into the universities and by the foundation of teachers' training colleges. In 1847 Tennyson published his dream of *The Princess*, that curious blend of medievalism and sentiment which, after a few fine passages of rhetoric, ends in the fashionable submission of the rebels and the masculine invocation: "Lay thy sweet hands in mine and trust to me." In 1862 Frances Power Cobbe read a paper before the Social Science Congress on the subject of women in the universities. It caused "unusual ridicule," and no prince invited her to make the graceful gesture of self-abnegation. But five years later, in spite of discouragement by women as intelligent as Charlotte M. Yonge, a committee was formed to found a college at which women could work for the Cambridge University Examinations. To-day the story of Miss Emily Davies and Girton reads curiously. She would not have her college inside Cambridge because of the difficulty of chaperonage and the possibilities of scandal. When in 1871 Miss Clough brought five girls actually into the town and founded Newnham, she was shocked, as Miss Beale had been when Miss Davies insisted upon examinations. But she was certain of one thing; she would tolerate no separate curriculum. The tests of masculine and feminine intelligence must be identical, or it would be impossible to gain recognition of their essential equality. In 1876 the Oxford and Cambridge Joint Board examinations were thrown open to women; two years later the Maria Grey Training College for women teachers was established, and in the same year London University was given its new charter, offering women, both students and teachers, precisely the same status as men.

This was regarded as an unparalleled victory. Since then though the older universities still reserve certain distinctions, though women were not admitted as full members of Oxford University till 1920, and are not at Cambridge till this day, the new universities made at least no statutory discrimination against them. Halls and hostels for women, training colleges for teachers, women members of university senates and commissions—these are the creations of the past half-century. To-day the standard of teaching in girls' schools on all subjects except mathematics, science and classical languages, is as high as and sometimes higher than that in boys', and many of the new methods in education—the Dalton Plan, the Montessori system, the Macmillan project of open-air nursery schools —have been the work of women teachers.

But the third obstacle remains. There is still a weight of tradition and home influence oppressing both the school-girl and her teacher. The Hadow Report commented upon the amount of work in the home to be done by girls at secondary schools. In elementary schools this is equally true, though here it is slightly counterbalanced by the fact that rather more boys than girls do pre-school jobs, delivering milk and papers and the like. Still, girls not only do these recognised jobs; they mind babies, push prams and "run out to the shop for mother." In those private boarding-schools which still exist for the well-to-do girl, repeatedly the parents' influence counteracts all that the teachers may do to prepare her for life as a rational human being. In colleges and technical schools, the burden not only of domestic responsibility but of masculine dis-couragement lies heavily on the woman student. Poverty handicaps her; the conflicting claims of family and pro-fessional duties rend her; tradition, centuries-old, bids her subordinate the demands of her inquiring mind to the interests of her seniors. Because of these handicaps, the vindication of woman's intelligence is not yet quite accomplished. The instruments lie to her hands, but the freedom to use them is not yet wholly hers.

The Vindication of Personality

It was all very well for women to claim equal citizenship and equal educational advantages. Neither reform could touch the roots of their trouble so long as that conception of personality, upon which ethical standards are based, remained in question. The fight for an equal moral standard, which came to be recognised as part of the Woman's Movement in the nineteenth century, was not merely the work of Puritan cranks actuated by dislike for what they thought to be sexual immorality. It was and is an essential aspect of women's claim to full humanity.

Throughout the nineteenth century, women were toasted as "The Ladies"; "the ladies" were "the sex," and sex (when it was not comic) was indecent. The jocular references to the "fair sex" which still inspire musical jokes, after-dinner speeches and smoke-room stories are only echoes of the mingled humour and ribaldry with which all early innovations in female activity—from preaching at Methodist meetings to studying higher mathematics—were regarded. This attitude had the double effect of increasing the psychological difficulties of pioneer women, and of making it harder than ever for the public to take their efforts seriously.

So long as men regard women, and women regard themselves, not as persons but as adjuncts of somebody else's vice or honour, all human relationships must be awry. The personality of the wife must be subordinate to her husband's desire. The passing of the Married Women's Property Act was a superficial benefit compared with the refusal to tolerate the conception of marital morality which found expression in Luther's maxim: "If a woman becomes weary or at last dead from bearing, that matters not; let her only die from bearing, she is there to do it." Political enfranchisement only set an instrument for reform into the hands of women whose security of chastity and monogamy was purchased by the outlawry of the prostitute. It was she of whom, in 1869, the historian Lecky felt obliged to write, "Herself the supreme type of vice, she is ultimately the most efficient guardian of virtue." The improvement of schools for girls could not alone counteract the effects of a less fortunate type of education which they might receive though indecent assault, procuration, and those other offences against the person which, until the 1920's, were treated by the law as of less importance than minor offences against property. Nor could alleviation of the severity with which illicit unions were penalised by society, remedy the injustice done to illegitimate children whose prospects in life were artificially handicapped as a recompense for what was held to be the anti-social conduct of their parents. The whole problem of woman's labour, in the home, in industry, and in the professions, was equally complicated by this undercurrent of emotion concerning her sexual frailty. Because of this, women medical students were banned from certain hospitals because they might embarrass their male colleagues when attending lectures on anatomy; night-work was thought unsafe for women industrial workers, who must walk to it through the perilously tempting darkness. Beneath the controversy surrounding the paid employment of married women lies the traditional gulf between the celibate woman engaged in non-domestic work, and the married woman employed solely in the home, a tradition which gained force not only from conventual memories, but from the ancient doctrine that a wife should have no interests and indeed no independent personality apart from her husband.

So closely interwoven with all common actions was the code of patriarchal morality, dating from the Roman Empire, from the Hebrew pilgrimage in the wilderness, from the supremacy, perhaps, of the old man gnawing his bones in the paleolithic cave, that it left its trace upon every aspect of a European woman's life; while the harem system, the sati ideal, the slave morality of Asia and of Africa, contributed their quota of influence to female status. And if it was true that these traditions affected the ethical values of Western civilisation, it was equally true that current personal morality appeared to depend upon those traditions. "With the repudiation of the patriarchal subordination of women," wrote one anthropologist quite recently, "the whole edifice of traditional Western sexual morality collapses." Hence the tenacity with which many respectable men and women clung to customs in themselves barbarous, archaic and unjustifiable by reason; because, if the customs vanished, the great ethical edifice of monogamy, home and family, might disappear. It was this clinging to discredited custom for the sake of what was thought to be safety, that led Josephine Butler in 1897 to write that "our race is suffering largely from a species of moral atrophy, from a fatal paralysis of the sense of justice."

Ethical standards enter more intimately into human lives than political principles. They strike at nerves and memory and imagination, transforming character and dominating affection; they colour opinions upon matters which seem superficially to have no connection with them. The attempt to change morality, therefore, was more subtle, difficult and painful than any other challenge made as part of the women's movement. The real battle was fought privately in a thousand homes, unchronicled and obscure. It centred round the refusal of women to tolerate adultery as a trivial offence for husbands but a capital crime for wives. It centred round the insistence of self-respecting women that they had the right to give or withhold their bodies in love according to their own principles of conduct, and not the arbitrary will of their legal guardians. It centred round the determination of women to be recognised as persons in themselves, not merely the repositories of a man's honour or his "sin."

But in public it found its principle expression in the campaign against the Contagious Diseases Act identified with the name of Josephine Butler. The state regulation of prostitution was part of Napoleon's brilliant legacy of order to Europe. Its justification was that it made the physical relief of copulation safer and easier—especially for soldiers. If prostitutes could be medically examined and brothels licensed, venereal disease, an increasingly grave problem during the social upheaval of the Napoleonic Wars, might be checked. In France and other parts of Europe the system appeared to work admirably; it was a little unfortunate that even medical inspection, arbitrary, compulsory and brutal as it might become, was never fool-proof; but at least the governments instituting it might feel that they had done their best to make the world safe for virility. It was unfortunate, too, that opinion was not unanimous about the comfort and convenience of regulated brothels. When, in 1860, a commission discussed the question of their provision for India, Florence Nightingale gave evidence against them, and Harriet Martineau had the indelicacy to write articles against them in the *Daily News*. Being plain, deaf, and a Unitarian, Miss Martineau's lack of decorum, though deplored, was not considered fatal.

In 1864, '66, '68 and '69 by laws known as the Contagious Diseases Acts, the system was introduced into England; but the opposition was stiffening. In 1869 a woman who was neither the heroine of the Crimea nor a deaf political economist attacked the policy; she was Mrs. Josephine Butler, a happily-married mother of a beloved family, rich in the possession of wealth, culture, popularity and great personal beauty; but who, after the sudden death of a daughter, turned to consider the condition of society and found its treatment of prostitution its darkest stain. In 1870 she founded the Ladies' Association whose ultimate object was the achievement of an equal moral standard for men and women.

This organisation split the feminist movement; it outraged society; it caused riots; it held all-night prayer meetings. Its objects were the punishment of seduction, the introduction of equal legislation for men and women, the amendment of the bastardy laws and the repeal of the Contagious Diseases Acts. The arguments urged against the Acts were the cause of the sharpest outcry; it surprised people to hear the gentle and beautiful Mrs. Butler protest that "the odium of all Regulation of Public Immorality is aimed at and confined to women"; that state regulation of prostitution meant state outlawry and public bullying of prostitutes; that if women could be penalised for "soliciting" it was unjust not to penalise their partners in the act which followed upon solicitation. After sixteen years of vigorous campaigning, the Contagious Diseases Acts were repealed. But the struggle against them had taught the campaigners more about the social system upon which civilised morality was based than they found it tolerable to know.

In England, seduction of a child of thirteen or over was not punishable, if the man could claim that she had consented to the act. Procuring was not an indictable offence. Prostitutes could be punished, but pimps and *souteneurs* were honourable citizens. In 1881 a commission investigated the enticement of girls for purposes of prostitution known as the White Slave Traffic and drafted a Criminal Law Amendment Bill; but could not get it passed. Always when it came up before the House of Commons it was blocked or talked out, as similar reforms have been on various occasions before and since. Because it concerned wrongs inflicted upon the unenfranchised, it had no political importance. Only in 1885, after the sensational case of W. T. Stead's prosecution and imprisonment on a technical judgment (when, to prove the truth of his articles, *The Maiden Tribute of Modern Babylon*, he bought from her mother a girl of thirteen, kept her for the night in a brothel and conveyed her out of London), was the Bill which had been delayed during four years rushed through both Houses of Parliament in five days.

But that was only the beginning. The abolition of regulated prostitution in England did not put an end to the system in the British Empire. From 1912 to 1932 a series of enactments throughout the Crown Colonies abolished regulation there—from Colombo to Hong Kong. But still in Queensland and parts of India, brothels are licensed. In other countries not only are brothels licensed and prostitutes compulsorily examined, but the system leads to a constant trade in the ignorance and poverty of girls who, in order to supply the continuous demand, must be deceived into entering a profession to which even economic extremity would not willingly drive them. The repugnance of normal women for prostitution is proved by this—that for no other calling is it necessary to organise an immense secret international kidnapping service, such as that revealed in 1927 and 1932 by the League of Nations' Reports upon the White Slave Traffic.

The campaign against these conditions is by no means completed. In almost every country prostitutes are considered as a race apart, beyond the ordinary protection o the law extended to their customers. In New York two years ago the report of the Seabury investigations into the magistrates' courts revealed a "ring of conspiracy, blackmail and intimidation between the police and the magistrates" so corrupt and brutal that it led to the dissolution of the Anti-Vice and Law Enforcement Committee. In spite of the effort of the League of Nations' Committees upon the traffic in women, and their constant assertion that the traffic cannot be suppressed so long as certain states legalise *maisons de tolerance*, brothels are still licensed; girls are still procured. In China child slaves are still sold for prostitution; slave dhows still carry negresses across the Red Sea for sale in Arabia; child marriages in India, in North Africa, in Persia, the celebrated Red Light Squares of Buenos Ayres; the heavier penalisation of women than men for adultery wherever it is practised; Lord Trenchard's recent "cleaning up" of the London streets by driving prostitutes from their familiar beats—all these are only symptoms of the same attitude, and protests against them are based upon the same principles. In almost every civilised country there are organisations national and international, at work for the establishment of an equal moral standard.

The commercial exploitation of prostitution may be the

crudest, but it is not the only violation of personality resulting from the standard of values which counts women as ancillary to the interests of men. Luther's observation about child-bearing referred to married women. The extreme distress and isolation penalising "immodest" conduct affected the sheltered daughters of respectable parents. Under a code of morals which, as in the middle of the nineteenth century, regarded the exposure of an ankle as an act of indiscretion, or advised a pregnant woman to prepare for delivery by wearing an old flannel petticoat in order that the doctor might not be embarrassed by unnecessary exposure of her body, the protection of chastity became a social obsession.

While one effect of this ethical disproportion was to handicap all natural activities of women outside the home, a second result was to delay scientific investigation and popular enlightenment about those very functions upon which female attention was compulsorily concentrated. The ignorance and superstition which in 1934 still surround the subject of sex; the difficulties faced by those who, since Charles Bradlaugh and Mrs. Annie Besant were prosecuted in 1876 for circularising an American pamphlet *The Fruits of Philosophy*, have concerned themselves with research into and popularisation of the subject of contraception; the sentimentality still transfusing all discussions of the population question; the comparative neglect of infant welfare; the lack of interest displayed by public authorities in the creation and preservation of healthy human life compared with the provision of military defence against possible enemies—all these varying aspects of modern life arise from the same deeply-rooted conviction that women and their affairs are of less importance than men and their affairs. A modern state thinks it essential to have three full ministries—one each to organise military, naval and air destruction—but only one ministry of health, for the preservation of life. New battleships are readily ordered, when clinics, school meals, and ante-natal provision are counted as "extravagance." Being identified with "women's interests" they are held to be of second-rate public importance. The attempt to re-adjust these values made ever since women in the middle of the last century asserted their right to some voice in public affairs, is part of the vindication of personality. Though at first glance the connection is not evident, the same belief in the significance of common humanity made Margaret Macmillan hurl her passionate claim for nursery schools against the armoured indifference of the London County Council, and Josephine Butler attack all licensed brothels.

Connected in the same struggle have been individual campaigns for reform of specific injustices and inequalities. When after the war some former suffrage workers asked why it was still necessary for women to organise, the answer came from societies such as the Six Point Group, the National Union of Societies for Equal Citizenship, and the National Council for the Unmarried Mother and her Child, that the law still regarded too lightly the human personality when its sex was female. In 1919 a new agitation began for tightening up the laws concerning offences against children, resulting in 1922 in the Criminal Law Amendment Act, passed through the House of Commons at two o'clock in the morning, after a vain attempt to "talk it out" as irrelevant to public welfare. In 1924 a Home Office Committee was appointed to inquire into Sexual Offences against Young Persons. Its recommendations have not yet been made law, though in December, 1931, the violation and murder of a London girl of ten, Vera Page, startled the public conscience and led to the appointment of a committee by thirteen voluntary organisations to consider the further strengthening of the law and administration.

It was the knowledge that the death-rate among illegitimate children doubled that of those born in wedlock, as much as the injustice done to unmarried mothers, which led to the various attempts made to improve their position. In 1872 a law was passed in England, making a father liable to contribute 5s. a week to maintain his illegitimate child. In 1918 the Affiliation Orders (Increase of Maximum Payment) Act raised the sum to 10s.; the Legitimacy Act of 1927 legitimised a child if its parents subsequently married, neither being married to other persons at the time of its conception. Since then a Bastardy Bill introduced by Lord Astor has proposed further alleviation of the unmarried mother's position. The further amendment of the Divorce Laws followed the same principle of equality between the sexes—the idea behind all these reforms being that morality is not secured by terrorism, and that its surest safeguard is the treatment of women as equal and adult human beings.

The more recent campaign in Europe and America, associated with the names of Mrs. Margaret Sanger, Dr. Marie Stopes, Councillor Margaret Ashton, and Mrs. How Martyn, for scientific improvement of contraceptive methods, and public provision of facilities for their proper use, is equally part of the same process. The nineteenth century preached the sanctity of motherhood, but withheld from women crippled by over-frequent pregnancies, the knowledge which would enable them to produce healthy children at calculable intervals. It preached wifely submission, even if its fruits might be economic or physical catastrophe. Better risk death and the consequent ills which befall a motherless family, than withhold from a husband his conjugal rights or take measures to render them innocuous. Out of the primeval twilight of racial memory, we preserved the consciousness that sex is a perilous power, and that women possess fierce magic, dangerous to men and yet essential to their comfort; in return Nature has burdened women with the unadjustable, unpredictable accident of pregnancy. To change a gamble with fortune into a deliberate act subject to human will threatened a drastic upheaval of age-old expectation. If women were no longer subject to that instability, that dependence upon circumstance, which might at any moment visit them in the helplessness of late pregnancy and childbirth, they could plan their lives and calculate possibilities with assurance equal to that of their male colleagues, and yet not buy this freedom with celibacy. The whole nature of women's attitude towards life, their place in society, their capacity and self-confidence could be changed. Instead of waiting upon time and tide and the rhythm of life's creative current; instead of accepting meekly the reiterated annunciation—"Behold the handmaid of the Lord; be it unto me according to thy word"—they could challenge chance and circumstance, fortune and misfortune, as well as any other human creature. Their mood might change from passive to active participation in life.

It is impossible to over-emphasise the psychological importance of this movement. It is still in its infancy. Only a few women in a few countries to-day understand and practise birth-control. Methods are not infallible. It casts an odd reflection upon masculine tradition that, though the contraceptive methods practised by men are simpler, cheaper and safer, it is for the instruction of women that clinics must be founded.

In this country the Ministry of Health has given permission for local authorities to set up clinics where information can be given to married women; but it remains the choice of the authorities whether they will do so. In Russia information is available; but contraceptives are so scarce that the more drastic remedy of abortion is frequently adopted. In Sweden, Norway and Denmark clinics are permitted and a certain number have been established. In Spain the practice or teaching of contraceptive methods are permitted by law since the revolution, but actually little has been done. In many other countries, such as

France, Italy and Ireland the teaching of contraceptive methods is still a penal offence. The Catholic tradition exercises a formidable counter-influence.

Yet the organisations conducting this campaign are, consciously or unconsciously, fighting the battle of the equal moral standard. They are making possible the independent and self-confident facing of the future by women who have hitherto been pawns of destiny—happy pawns most often, unaware of the inconvenience of their position, sometimes indeed enjoying its uncertainties; but pawns, nevertheless. They are taking part in a revolution of which the fruits will be ethical and psychological as well as biological and economic; but the full nature of which we can still only prophesy by hazard.

The Right to Work

The Marxian doctrine of the economic interpretation of history may go too far; but it was not Lenin, it was Josephine Butler, who declared that "Economics lie at the very root of practical morality." The vindication of personality claimed by women during the past hundred and fifty years would have remained purely academic had they secured no increase of economic independence. When Caroline Norton asserted her innocence of the "criminal conversations" alleged against her by her husband, her sole means of support were her rather precarious literary earnings; yet she was not legally entitled even to these. A less spirited woman with less influential friends, would have been completely helpless before a system of law which denied her every right of citizenship and property. In similar circumstances other deserted wives were driven to a domestic service little removed from economic slavery, or to the prostitution which involved temporal if not eternal damnation.

Before the industrial revolution women had their secure if subordinate part in the economic life of the country.

As wives, they had the wide range of domestic industry; unmarried, they took part in the varied activities of household, farm or home manufacture. It is true that their industrial prestige had dwindled since the Middle Ages when as members of crafts guilds they had a place in the organisation of industry; that under Queen Elizabeth's Act of 1562 female paupers could be compelled to enter domestic service under threat of imprisonment; that the growing complexity of processes and division of labour were, from the seventeenth century onwards, removing the old crafts of spinning, weaving, leather-curing, and brewing from the home to the specialist's workshop; that the middle-class woman was learning to ape the parasitism of the leisured lady; but not until the nineteenth century did woman's place in the economic life of this, or indeed any other, nation become the problem that it has been ever since.

The claim of the right to work was a claim to something more fundamental than the chance of earning an independent income. Society had never denied the biological utility of woman; hitherto it had seen no reason to deny her economic utility as a producer. But now the forces that urged the claim to recognised citizenship and to wider education were prompting the more intellectually alert and ambitious women to demand opportunity for the full exercise of their powers. Women wanted to be doctors, lawyers and administrators, as well as teachers, actresses and novelists. The restricted field hitherto open to them was not wide enough. Queen's College, founded for the training of governesses, reared also the tempestuous and indomitable Sophia Jex Blake, whose courageous siege of the fortresses of Edinburgh and London opened the medical profession to women in England. In 1870 the London School of Medicine for Women was founded. Florence Nightingale had already reorganised the nursing profession. Cornelia Sorabji, fifteen years later, was the first woman to be admitted to the Oxford law examinations. By 1911

Olive Schreiner was able to speak for her generation in *Woman and Labour*, as Mary Wollstonecraft a hundred years earlier, had spoken for hers. But Olive Schreiner's plea was not a cry for "rights," it was a demand for opportunities. "We take all labour for our province! From the judge's seat to the legislator's chair; from the statesman's closet to the merchant's office; from the chemist's laboratory to the astronomer's tower, there is no part or form of toil for which it is not our intention to attempt to fit ourselves; and there is no closed door we do not intend to force open; and there is no fruit in the garden of knowledge it is not our determination to eat."

The process of women's entry into new forms of economic activity was temporarily accelerated by the war of 1914-1918. Then, owing to shortage of male labour, women became engineers, registrars, and bankers; they punched tram tickets, entered the police force, ran racing-studs, and practised veterinary surgery. In 1919 the Sex Disqualification (Removal) Act was intended to clear away all remaining artificial barriers between women and their complete occupational freedom. The feminists and professional women had no doubt what they wanted—freedom to qualify themselves, equal opportunities with men, a fair field and no favour. The arguments in favour of identical examinations for both sexes urged by Miss Davies and her contemporaries were repeated by the spokesmen of organised professional women in the twentieth century.

But the whole movement was not straightforward nor simple. Professional women might know clearly enough what they wanted. The lecturer's desk, the astronomer's observatory, the surgeon's operating-table are places where men and women alike, if their tastes incline them that way, desire to stand. Provided that an income is forthcoming from somewhere, the work has fascination enough to attract experts to perform it without hope of payment; just as artists will paint pictures and violinists play sonatas, for love of their craft. All that the women wanted was to be allowed to work as much, as well, and as effectively as they could.

But the case of the industrial woman was rather different. There are women as well as men to-day who enjoy their hours in mill or laundry. The skilled worker takes pleasure in his job. The clean modern buildings, the sense of comradeship, the respite from bickering, overcrowding and discomfort which are too frequently the dominating experiences of the "home"—the sense of earning money, the independence, the chance of promotion—all these have made some women relish with gusto even monotonous factory labour. In *Memoirs of the Unemployed* published in 1934, a skilled "perm-winder" in the weaving-department of an artificial silk factory calls hers "a grand job." Unemployed, after nine years there, she declared. "I hate this nothing-to-do. I am a strong woman and I can keep this little house clean with two hours' work a day. I liked having my work at the factory, although it meant eleven hours away from home every day and five on Saturday, and doing the cooking, washing, and sewing for the week on Saturday afternoon and Sunday. But I liked doing it, and I worked hard for the regular 30s." She was a married woman with six children, deserted ten years previously by her husband. Her sturdy independence and enjoyment of life are characteristic of the north-country textile-workers. In the modern factories of Bournville, York, Welwyn, and other centres of improved equipment and modernised methods, there are many such women employees who really find satisfaction in their work comparable to the satisfaction of the professional and business woman.

But there are, of course, still far too many wretchedly paid and organised trades. The tailoresses of East London who at the opening of 1934 were on strike in Bethnal Green, the dressmakers' apprentices, "polishers," and "finishers," all the low-grade ranks of semi-skilled and unskilled labour have been little affected by modern methods of hygiene, labour-saving and welfare; though even their conditions have been slightly alleviated by the Trade Boards, Shops Acts and Factory Acts.

At the end of the eighteenth century, however, when the factory system was first instituted, there could be little pleasure or pride in industrial work.

Dominated by the *laissez-faire* theories of the Manchester School, employers saw nothing anti-social in the practice of buying labour in the cheapest market. Pauper children from the poor-law institutions were best of all; but when the supply of small half-starved boys and girls proved unobtainable or inadequate, women were the next best substitutes.

Such women did not enter industry for choice; they were driven in as an alternative to starvation for themselves and their families. Often they could obtain employment when there was none for their fathers and husbands. Labour was unregulated, workers' organisation forbidden, wages as low as competition could force them.

In such circumstances women were paid less than men. A Government report of 1834 gives the maximum wages in the Lancashire cotton industry as 22s. 8½d. for men, and 9s. 8¼d. for women. That ratio was customary and considered to be perfectly proper.

The reasons justifying this were traditional. Women's economic position was less secure than men's. It was presumed, often inaccurately, that they had no families to support. It was argued that owing to marriage and pregnancy their work was less regular and reliable; their muscular strength was generally less, though with the growing use of machinery this distinction became of decreasing importance, until the Report of the Women's Employment Committee of 1919 stated: "The progress of scientific equipment is fast replacing strength by dexterity. Women's future industrial kingdom, therefore, is hardly

73

limited by her weaker muscles, for this is a boundary which is disappearing." The same committee also observed the superiority of the masculine hand and brain for industrial processes to be largely a matter of training.

But a hundred years ago women had small chance to prove their natural capacity. The factories themselves were little hells of discomfort. In their opposition to the Factory Acts the proprietors of linen mills protested that it was good for women to work in an atmosphere of 120 to 140 degrees; but John Roebuck, M.P., in 1838 described to his wife a Scottish cotton mill in which women, "young, all of them, some large with child . . . were obliged to stand twelve hours each day. . . . The heat was excessive in some of the rooms, the stink pestiferous, and in all an atmosphere of cotton flue. I nearly fainted." After twelve or even fourteen hours spent thus, the workers returned to their crowded hovels and tenements of industrial slums, without water supply, lighting, heating or sanitation, where there were neither taps, nor sinks nor drainage. Small wonder that their health was exhausted, carrying the double burden of domestic and industrial labour against such handicaps.

Therefore from the beginning of the factory system, women's work was considered, and often was, inferior to that of men; their health was worse; their temperament more docile. Generations of submission lay behind them, and generations of maternal responsibility. Though in a sermon of 1853 the Reverend Charles Gutch of Leeds spoke of the "vice and profaneness, the unchecked profligacy, the unblushing wickedness" of the workpeople in a certain mill, and considered the appalling agony following an explosion a fitting recompense for iniquity, for the most part the women worked to keep their children. An inspector's report of 1844 declared: "A vast majority of the persons employed at night and for long hours during the day are females. Their labour is cheaper and they are more easily induced to undergo severe bodily fatigue than men, either from the praiseworthy motive of gaining additional support for their families or from the folly of satisfying a love of dress."

Therefore, from their entry into industry, women were compulsory blacklegs, and the men of 1834 liked being displaced from their jobs no more than the men of 1934. In more than one town there were riots against female labour. One working man suggested complaining to the Prince Consort. A gentleman called W. R. Grey wrote a serious essay called *Why are Women Redundant?* In 1841 a deputation of working men petitioned Mr. Gladstone for "the gradual withdrawal of all females from the factories," maintaining that "home, its cares and its employments, is woman's true sphere." Owing to the expansion of empire following the Napoleonic Wars and the subsequent large-scale emigration of colonists, the excess of women over men in the population was almost as noticeable as it is to-day. Even when the women had displaced no men, the large numbers of them hurrying to the mills in the early morning, swinging five abreast, arm in arm, down the narrow streets on a Saturday evening, displaying their best bonnets for chapel on a Sunday, all created the illusion that England was full of wage-earning women taking the bread from the mouths of honest men.

Therefore over industrial employment, men and women appeared to be driven into competition as they had never been before, and a very natural masculine reaction was to attempt the restriction of women's field of employment and reduction of their competitive powers wherever possible.

But this is not all. The conditions of industrial labour in those early days were appalling. In spite of the natural callousness of man confronted by conditions which he thinks inevitable, and which are justified by economic theories considered incontestable, there were men and women whose social conscience could not tolerate the spectacle of social misery, the stunted child workers, the wretched dwellings, the squalor and indecency revealed in such documents as the 1842 Report on Mines and Collieries, when women and children (as the cheapest and most docile form of labour) were described as dragging trucks of coal, harnessed like dogs by a chain and girdle, through underground passages in which they had to creep on hands and knees, half naked, filthy and exhausted. They felt that something must be done, yet they were deterred by the *laissez-faire* theorists of the Manchester School, who were shocked by any suggestion of interference with the free play of labour demand and supply, and prophesied disastrous results from any attempt to regulate the free agency of adult employees. It was during the battles between pity and poverty, theory and sentiment, fought round the Factory Acts during the first half of the nineteenth century, that the ingenious solution was discovered, of reckoning women as non-adult and classifying them in a special category with children and growing persons.

This solution has dominated all subsequent industrial legislation, affected the entire position of women's employment, and led to one of the most bitter economic controversies of the twentieth century—the quarrel over Restrictive Legislation.

In 1802 Sir Robert Peel brought in the first of all Factory Acts, "The Health and Morals of Apprentices Bill" concerned entirely with children. But when in 1844 the hours of work for young persons were limited to twelve, women were also included. Women, with children, were prohibited from underground work in mines. When, in 1901 previous factory legislation was consolidated, the Home Secretary was empowered to make regulations concerning dangerous trades, most of which applied to women and children; women's hours were specially limited; their night-work was curtailed. Since then, further English laws of 1907, 1909, 1916, 1920 and 1926 have subjected women's labour, with that of adolescents, to restrictions which do not apply to men. Women, not men, are "protected" by these laws, may not with certain exceptions work on Sundays or during the night; women have specially limited overtime; women must take their meals simultaneously, have seats provided for them, and not remain in the factory during meal-times. Under the Factory and Workshops Act of 1910 they are prevented from following certain occupations. They may not cast brass, manipulate lead colour, use paint containing white lead, nor be employed as glost-placers in potteries. In many industries and a large number of professions, including teaching and the Civil Service, the majority of women are compelled to resign their posts on marriage.

When the International Labour Organisation was founded by the Treaty of Versailles "the protection of children, young persons and women" was specially mentioned in the list of objects recorded in its preamble. Its first annual conference drew up conventions concerning women's employment before and after childbirth, during the night and in unhealthy processes, and many countries have followed this demarcation. On the other hand, nations with highly civilised labour conditions have rejected it. Denmark has laws regulating women's industrial work before and after childbirth; but the proposal to ratify the Geneva Night Work Convention was opposed by women, and the Eight-Hour Day regulations apply to both sexes. Holland which had special restrictive laws for women till 1919 abolished the distinction between the sexes then, by making them apply to men as well. Iceland, Norway and Spain have special provisions only for maternity, and after constant agitation by women's organisations the International Labour Office is being persuaded to reconsider the terms of its Night Work Convention.

77

If women have special treatment under the laws, they are also handicapped by trade union regulations. Worse paid, worse organised, obstructed by domestic responsibilities, by prejudice against "those go-to-meetings-women" as one witness put it, and by their own frequent belief that employment was merely a stop-gap until marriage, they have been in a weaker position for bargaining than men. Paid at lower rates, they could only make smaller contributions to the union funds. Consequently it is not surprising that they have from the beginning played a subordinate part in trade union organisation, that they are frequently shut out from membership, and often excluded from well-paid and highly-skilled processes. In this country they are forbidden to smelt metal by the Iron and Steel Trades Confederation. The Amalgamated Association of Beamers, Twisters and Drawers-in will not allow them to take part in those occupations. They may not enter the Amalgamated Cotton Spinners Association as spinners, though they may become "piercers" or assistants. They are excluded from certain grades of high-class tailoring, cutting, printing and book-binding.

From the 1830's till this day there are people who declare that women need, for their own welfare, these special restrictions. The humanitarians, moved by the sight of woman's suffering, the sentimentalists who regard her chiefly as a potential mother, the male trade unionists, jealous of their own standards, and certain sections of women themselves, such as the Standing Joint Committee of Industrial Women's Organisations, which, in spite of the middle-class origin of its most articulate members, claims to represent the organised opinion of working women, maintain that differential sex legislation has not harmed women, that, for instance, in the textile industries of Lancashire, the most highly skilled and highly paid women themselves demand it, that women caught between starvation and oppression cannot be reached as free agents, and that after conditions have been alleviated for women, the improvements are extended to men.

But from the middle of the last century this opinion has been contested. When the Short Hours Bill of 1872 was introduced women took no part in the agitation and suffrage leaders protested against unequal restrictions based upon sex difference. The Women's Trade Union League of 1877 founded largely through the enterprise of Emma Patterson, stood for the equal treatment of men and women and urged women to organise in their own trade unions. When in 1882 a Bill was introduced prohibiting girls under fourteen from acting as blacksmiths, the Women's Trade Union League asked that the restrictions should apply to boys as well. Six years later, Clementina Black, of the Women's Trades Council, proposed at the Trades Union Council that "where women do the same work as men, they shall receive equal pay," and her seconder, Mrs. Juggins of the Midland Trades Federation, said that nothing but equal pay could help the women. The 1885 Coal Mines Regulation (Amendment) Act, started the now notable controversy about the Pit-brow lassies, some of whom marched proudly to Westminster to demonstrate their physical ability. But not until the twentieth century did the controversy reach its climax when, round the abortive Factory Bill of 1924, the whole issue of differential *versus* equal regulation for male and female labour agitated the Press, gave birth to new national and international organisations, tore one celebrated society from end to end, and cleft a deep division between "protectionists" and "equalitarians."

For the equalitarians believed that special regulation, advocated as privilege became disability. They saw that women's pay remained sometimes half, sometimes two-thirds the rate of men's. The Trade Boards standardised wages at the weekly rate of 48s. 10d. for men and 27s. 6d. for women. The Burnham Scale fixed women's rates at four-fifths that of men. They believed that special "privileges" for women, such as the prohibition of night work, or the clause of the 1926 Factory Bill forbidding women to clean machinery in motion, tended to debase the rate of wages still lower, by making women's labour more expensive.

They saw too that the differential rules still further restricted the possible fields of women's employment. After the Geneva Night-Work Convention had been passed, women electrical engineers protested that a promising career was cut short for female supervisors, since electricity is naturally needed most at night. From the Home Office report of 1919 it was clear that many processes in flour-milling, sugar-refining, gas-manufacture, paint works, and light leather works where women during the war had worked satisfactorily, were closed to them owing to regulations forbidding work at night or on Sundays.

It was Mrs. Emma Patterson who pointed out also that special regulations made the organisation of women workers even more difficult than it would have been otherwise, and that it limited opportunities for their industrial training.

The equalitarians claimed that the classification with young persons did no good to the general body of workers either. So far as children and young persons were concerned, the further their interests were separated from those of adult workers, the better. Children should be regarded as future citizens rather than as wage-earners. They claimed too that the special "protection" of women, in the end did little service to male workers. The original hope of some reformers was that regulations applied first to women should subsequently be extended to men. But until 1891 no "interference" with male adult labour was attempted, and afterwards the exclusion of women from certain dangerous processes frequently has been made an excuse for delaying further amelioration. This was especially true of the lead paint controversy of 1926, when, without any proof that lead poisoning chiefly affected women (indeed, as a racial poison, plumbism is probably more often transmitted through fathers) both internationally at Geneva and then nationally in the various member states, instead of insisting on the more costly substitutes for white lead in certain processes, the employers and governments satisfied their consciences by excluding women from employment in them, and letting the men remain.

"It is true that there was full and unreserved recognition," wrote N. A. Mess in *Factory Legislation and its Administration*, "of the fact that men need to be protected as well as women. The Factory Acts and the regulations under them ought to be scrutinised to see where men lack protection given to women, and, unless there is some very good reason, the protection should be extended to them also. Has not a man eyes? Has not a man a nose? Has not a man feet? If the workshop is badly ventilated, will not his health be impaired? Is it good for him to be unnecessarily wet or cold? Does he not need rest and holidays?"

In her Minority Report of the War Cabinet Committee on the Employment of Women in 1919, Mrs. Sidney Webb stated: "There is no more reason for such occupational or standard rates being made to differ according to the workers' sex than according to their race, creed, height or weight."

It has been also felt that the "not quite adult" status of industrial women affects the entire position of women in society. It perpetuates the notion that they are not quite persons; that they are not able to look after themselves; to secure their own interests, to judge whether they are fit or unfit to continue employment after marriage, to enter certain trades, or to assume equal responsibility with men in the state. It fosters the popular fallacy that women are the weaker sex, physically and mentally, by encouraging the low standard of life which ensures such weakness. There is nothing like malnutrition for producing the traditional "feminine" delicacy, nor like anæmia for securing that irresponsibility, instability and subservience which are the reputed characteristics of women in low-paid industries. Further, the equalitarians have observed that it was only in well-paid processes, where women came into competition with men, that restrictions have been thought desirable. Charwomen have no statutory hours for meal times. There is no prohibition of night work for domestic servants. Nurses may lift heavy weights, and working mothers continue coal-carrying and floor-scrubbing through pregnancy till the first pangs of labour, and resume them as soon as they can put a foot to the ground.

So there has been constant and recurrent opposition to the artificial restriction of women's labour. National and international societies have been founded to carry on the struggle. The Open Door International and the Equal Rights International are symptomatic of the tendency both of legislation and its critics to spread across the frontiers of states and continents. The organisation of women teachers and women doctors to uphold equalitarian principles demonstrates the final solidarity of professional with industrial women. But still, in 1934, with the best intentions in the world, public authorities dismiss married women employees upon marriage; factories exclude them from special processes; unequal pay is given for equal work. Still in the sacred names of motherhood and chivalry, women are obstructed in their attempt to earn a living wage; and still, because of their lower pay, they undercut men, lower wage rates, and act as unwilling black-legs throughout industry.

The right to work is not yet fully vindicated; but by 1933 women had at least entered into a larger variety of occupations than seemed possible even thirty-three years earlier. Diplomacy and the Church are nominally both closed to English women; yet Russia, Spain, Norway, America and Bulgaria have opened their diplomatic services to women; the present Lady Muir, as Mlle. Stancioff, entered the Bulgarian Diplomatic Service, and was appointed to the Bulgarian Legation at Washington. Without official title, Miss Gertrude Bell, as Temporary Assistant Political Officer, acted as chief British representative in Iraq during the Great War. On July 15th, 1933, the first conference of the United Methodist Churches carried a resolution "That the existing ministries of women which involve a dedication of life service already approved by the conference shall be united and abscribed into a new order of Women's Ministry." Women may not yet be stockbrokers. In the summer of 1933 a London stockbroker, commenting upon a Bradford woman's desire to join her local Stock Exchange, said, "There is not the slightest chance of their ever being admitted to the floor because stock-broking is regarded as an unsuitable profession for women." "Ever" is a long way. On the other hand there are women engineers, huntsmen and aviators. A woman, Mrs. Hamilton, is director of the British Broadcasting Corporation, though the first attempt to employ a women announcer was soon abandoned. A woman holds the post of Inspector of University Lodgings at Cambridge. 77,000 women are employed in the Civil Service. In 1933 four women detectives were appointed full members of the Criminal Investigation Department at Scotland Yard. Since the War, women policemen in their blue uniforms have been a familiar sight down city streets. A woman chemist is Assistant Analyst to the Corporation of Barrow-in-Furness. At Liverpool University a woman has been appointed Honorary Lecturer in Oceanography. For the first time, in 1933 a woman qualified as weaving manageress in an English cotton mill.

The position is still confused, subject to local variations, complicated by sentiment, prejudice and tradition. But it becomes increasingly obvious that under a mechanical civilisation when muscular superiority is no longer of primary importance, there is almost no work which a woman cannot do if she wishes and if she is allowed.

The Right to Property

The right to earn is by no means the same thing as the right to wealth. In an ideal community the ownership of considerable property would not be an exceptional privilege. The case for equalisation of incomes, however practically difficult, is from the hedonistic point of view unanswerable. But the world in which, during the past century and a half, women have attempted to vindicate their humanity, has displayed few signs of that Platonic communism which would make variations of income unimportant.

In that world, wealth means power, and women have been poor. Of course there have been exceptions. Miss Angela Burdett, born in 1814 and admirably brought up according to nineteenth-century standards of excellence, inherited the great Coutts fortune from a step-grand-mother. The Married Women's Property Acts had not been passed in those days, and Miss Burdett refused the numerous proposals cast at the feet of the richest heiress in Europe, conducted her own immense organisation of philanthropy, and became, in 1871, Baroness Burdett Coutts of Highgate and Brookfield, "one of the very few examples," observes Mrs. Ray Strachey in *The Cause*, "of a peerage bestowed on a woman for any other service than that of being mistress to a king." Before her there had been wealthy widows and princesses; after her there were to be the daughters of rich men, the singers and cinema stars to whom public infatuation brought fantastic for-tunes, and the slowly increasing number of business and

84

professional women whose earnings raised them from the stage of competence to power.

But for the most part women were and are poor. Individually, few of them possess or control large fortunes. It may be that they actually spend more money upon themselves than men. The furs, the jewels, the orchids, the sumptuously furnished flats, the beauty treatments advertised in the smooth, glossy pages of luxury magazines have been designed to tempt the appetites of women. The sable standard of conspicuous consumption is theirs. But the money spent upon perfumes and entertainments and yachts and houseparties usually comes from husbands and fathers who seek, through their women, to assert their expenditure-prestige upon an impressionable world. The expenditure may be the woman's, but the kingdom, the power and the glory which it buys, are masculine privileges.

The woman who sets out to earn her own living is still expected to content herself with a modest £250 a year. Her expenses, after all, need not be great. The advertised "flatlets for professional women," residential clubs and hostels, are modest places, where supper eggs may be boiled over gas-rings and friends entertained at night to innocuous cups of cocoa. A happy legend exists that a woman has no dependents and therefore requires a lower salary than men who have families to keep. The continued proofs by closer analysis that this is an illusion have hardly altered the widespread conviction in the public mind. Since the War several surveys have been taken, one by Professor Bowley of the London School of Economics, who examined one-tenth of the working-class households in five typical industrial towns, and supplemented this by investigating one-fifth of the census sheets of seven other towns and boroughs, and found that of the male workers over twenty, 27 per cent. were bachelors or widowers without dependent children, 24 per cent. married and without dependent children under fourteen; while the evidence given before the Royal Commission on the Civil Service, and included by Miss Helena Normanton in her book, *Sex Differentiation in Salary*, states that among women with over 7 years' service, 37 per cent. had dependents, among women with over 10 years' service 41 per cent., while among older women with 15 years' service, 43 per cent. had dependents, and of those who had worked over 20 years, 84 per cent.

A second contributing cause to low payment is the idea, often transformed into a fact by the insistence of private employers and local authorities, that every woman will resign her work on marriage. "A small wage, some leisure and more freedom," wrote Sir Charles Cheers Wakefield in an immensely popular book *On Leaving School*, "is all that a young, intelligent and, above all, an attractive-looking girl demands from her job; the rest she hopes to be supplied a few years later by a generous husband."

There are a few professions, the stage, journalism, the law and certain branches of medicine where men and women receive equal pay for equal work, though in all but the first, opportunities are still by no means equal. When in 1933 a woman doctor died leaving an estate valued at £70,000, her fortune made a front-page news item in the national Press for several days. Most self-supporting women still wear what Vera Brittain has wittily called "The Five Pound Look," the docile appearance of the creature content to remain in an ancillary position, and at best to take down dictated letters from the head of the firm instead of taking them from the assistant accountant in the back office.

What is true of individual incomes is equally true of national expenditure. It is not merely that when employed by the state women are paid less—even in the Civil Service where a Government pledge to the contrary has been made and hitherto consistently broken—but as a natural corollary it has followed that in budgeting for national expenditure, the estimates for those interests traditionally supposed specially to concern women should become minor items. It is a circle which, if not vicious in intention, becomes so in effect. For instance women, receiving lower wages than men, contribute less to public funds—1s. 1d. compared with 1s. 6d. weekly towards unemployment insurance; hence the benefits received are in the ratio of 15s. to 12s. (and 10s. for married women) in cases of sickness; 15s. 3d. to 13s. 6d. in case of unemployment. Nor, under such a standard of values, is it surprising that the national expenditure in this country during 1929-30 on maternity and child welfare should be less than the amount spent upon the singularly useless sugar-beet subsidy, less by £200,000 than the Road Fund, less than the estimate set down for "Army Works Buildings and Lands."

Women then, as individuals and as a sex, are poor. And their poverty has odd incidental effects upon themselves and upon their whole position. To be poor in a society founded upon private property, means to be insecure, and insecurity breeds timidity. The traditional characteristics of the typical governess, her touchiness, her cringing to authority, her uncertain temper with domestic servants, her lack of vitality and charm, are as assuredly the symptoms of poverty as the traditional good manners of a duke are symptomatic of a lifetime of inbred self-assurance. There have been governesses of genius; there was Charlotte Brontë; there have been dukes without affability; there was the Victor of Waterloo. But in her enchanting essay *A Room of One's Own*, Virginia Woolf has explained once and for all how poverty and insecurity breed servility, breed conventionality, and strangle initiative and vigour and imaginative enterprise.

Poverty breeds physical as well as psychological weakness. In 1934, when the Nutrition Board of the British Medical Association has made all too clear that a large

percentage of our population in this country is living below
the line of nourishment adequate to maintain body and
mind in proper health, this weakness is not confined
to women alone. But in the sweated industries which still
survive in spite of the Trades Boards Acts, in the thousands
of working-class homes just on or below the "poverty
line," in all the precarious ranks of low-paid unskilled
labour as well as among the unemployed, women's
physique is undermined by malnutrition. Their blood is
poor; their teeth decay, their muscles grow flabby and
their hearts "lack tone"; they suffer from nerves and
indigestion, from pyorrhoea and insomnia, and neuralgia.
In the homes of the unemployed or underpaid, the mothers
are usually those who fare the worst, snatching a cup of
tea and slice of "bread and marge" while packing the
children off to school, or cutting the husband's lunch-
time sandwiches. Yet when, during the war, girls undertook industrial work for which they were well-paid, and,
in spite of a food shortage, were able to feed as they had
never fed before and rarely since, the Home Office
Memorandum on the "Substitution of Women in War
Munition Factories" was able to report in 1919 that
"women appear to find labouring work healthy and not
too fatiguing."

The reaction is not only upon individual women. When
groups of women wish to do anything, to build a college,
found a newspaper, or finance a flight round the world,
they are still faced by appalling difficulties. The history of
their struggles for education, for political enfranchisement,
for professional opportunity all over the world has been
handicapped by poverty. Now and then a great emotional
movement has struck gold out of the stones. When
Florence Nightingale returned from the Crimea, when
Mrs. Pankhurst after a hunger-strike appealed for the
W.S.P.U., women sold their jewels, pawned their watches,
and sacrificed their small luxuries of books, concerts,

travel or dress, to respond to the appeal. Wives exerted psychological blackmail over affectionate husbands. The minority who had wealth offered it.

But for the most part women's clubs and colleges and schools are poor enough. This does not only mean that a professional woman wanting to interview a client can rarely take him to the Carlton Grill and mellow his attitude towards life by oysters and champagne in the time-honoured fashion of masculine diplomacy; it means also that when a girl goes to college she has fewer chances of a scholarship; that when she leaves she has fewer chances of occupying an endowed research position, and fewer chances of finding a benevolent speculator to finance her projected enterprises.

Even when women have through inheritance received wealth, so heavily are the scales of tradition weighted against expenditure upon their own sex that, as likely as not, they may entirely ignore their opportunity for serving its interests. Whittaker's Almanack provides a list of "Principle Charitable Bequests of the Year." From the 1934 volume it appears that Mrs. Betty May Gray, of Hurlingham, bequeathing £60,000 to charity, left £7,500 to Toc H, £5,000 for the benefit of ex-sailors, soldiers, airmen and merchant-men, and £5,000 "for organisations for training boys to become worthy citizens of a great Empire." Mrs. Emily France Jackson, of Carshalton, similarly left £40,000 to ex-soldiers and sailors; Miss Mary Ann Smith of Hove, £3,000 to Miss Weston's work for soldiers and sailors; Miss Emma May Webb, of Torquay, £1,000 to Harrow School "for a scholarship or for the sports of the school." Not a single recognisable bequest to girls' public schools or sports or training in good citizenship, an odd manifestation of sex snobbery.

It is not only while preparing for a career that poverty handicaps. Given a modicum of intelligence, money breeds money; capital accumulates; sensible expenditure upon secretaries, travel, office equipment, entertaining, may rapidly double or treble a professional income. And such expenditure gives opportunity for making those contacts essential in professional or business life. If the woman barrister is spending her Saturday afternoons washing camisoles and answering her letters, instead of sending the former to a laundry, dictating the latter to a secretary, and motoring out to glean briefs on Sunningdale golf links— whose fault is it that her male colleagues collect the business?

It may not be right that briefs, commissions, offices, investment tips, honorary fellowships, and cabinet appointments should be picked up at luncheons, week-end country house-parties and club houses; in Russia to-day we are told it is no longer so—and all the better; but at present this is how things are done in Europe and America (to say nothing of India, Africa and Australia as well, so far as such business is done there at all). It is part of the ironical injustice of a capitalist system that lucrative deals can be put through moderately well in a good office, better still in the dining-room of a first-rate restaurant, best of all on the deck of a private yacht. And, with notable exceptions, the offices *de luxe*, the running accounts at the Ritz-Carlton, and the private yachts, do not belong to business or professional women.

Of course things have improved. The battle for the right to property was in part a battle against certain laws which prevented women from holding or acquiring property; in part it was a battle for a larger share of state expenditure; most of all, it was a battle against the point of view which sees little reason why women should require anything beyond "a small wage, some leisure and more freedom."

The legal reforms were the easiest to achieve because they were the most definite.

When laws are strict enough, they bring their own remedy.

It was Barbara Bodichon and her little group of Langham Place reformers who first aroused public opinion to the state of things which led to the passing of the Married Women's Property Acts. From the 1850's onwards they had pressed for recognition of the hardship done to women who supported husband and family upon money which they earned but might not own. The Bill of 1870 attacked this evil first—women might keep possession of what they earned. Everything else still belonged to their husbands. After that, it was more difficult than ever to find popular support for further reform. Petitions might be signed; the energetic Lydia Becker might organise, but men did not see why women should not trust their husbands. Fortunately for the agitators, the tradesmen, constantly defrauded by the trickery of the law, supported them. The lawyers, tactfully entertained by Mrs. Jacob Bright, found the technical problem fascinating. In 1882 the full Married Women's Property Bill was passed.

It has been said that this did more for women's lives than any extension of the franchise. Actually the two types of reform react upon each other. Both meant increase of power. Both increased self-confidence. Both left a heritage of anomaly and contradiction.

To-day the laws of property are weighted against husbands rather than against wives. A wife has no obligation to support her husband (though under the Means Test her earnings may deprive him of benefit). The husband is bound by law still to support his wife, to provide a home for her, and to pay her income tax. The husband is still liable for his wife's "torts"; if she libels a neighbour, or is convicted of reckless driving or causes an obstruction in the highway, he must pay the fine. The whole business of credit is still inconveniently complicated by the relics of the older system. To-day a wife can pledge her husband's credit so long as the tradespeople choose to trust her; the husband may find himself summoned on several counts, owing large sums of money which he has never spent. In the poorer quarters of industrial towns this often occurs; imprisonment for debt may follow, and the man, not the woman, goes to gaol.

Feminist organisations such as the Six Point Group are, in 1934, attempting to remedy these inequalities. They will probably succeed. The discriminations against men arise out of a system which for two millennia proved unjust to women. If the pendulum has temporarily swung over the other way, it is only for a moment.

And only in certain cases. The law of 1926 equalised the rights of inheritance between men and women to intestates' property; but landed estates and titles still go first to the eldest son, even if there are daughters older than he. A peeress in her own right, such as the present Countess Roberts or Viscountess Rhondda, is still a rarity in the state, and both of these peerages were given in peculiar circumstances for service by the fathers.

The fight for obtaining a full share of the national income was the latest to begin and is still proceeding. The National Health Insurance Act of 1911 certainly brought thousands of women within the scope of state insurance, but they neither paid equal contributions nor received equal benefits. For the same reasons, unemployment insurance perpetuated the same inequality. That was perhaps inevitable. So long as women earn less than men and are paid less, even for equal work, so long must their contributions to the common state—whether it be trade union fund, national insurance or political party subscription—be smaller, and their subsequent benefits less.

But a different principle has underlain two other movements—the post-war struggle for widows' pensions and the present campaign for some system of family allowances.

Both of these take for granted a social and economic system, whereby the family is dependent upon the husband and father, the woman abandons paid employment upon marriage, and the children do not become self-supporting until they have reached adolescence. Actually this is a comparatively modern state of affairs. As Eleanor Rathbone points out in her *Disinherited Family*, during the Middle Ages women worked as producers in the fields and home. Until the nineteenth century child-labour was taken for granted. A Statute of 1389 refers to a "child who has used husbandry till twelve." But as the humanitarian legislation and domestic custom of the nineteenth century drove first children and then a great majority of married women from the labour market, all became dependent upon the wage-earning householder. One consequence of this was that any accident to him became catastrophic to the family. A second was that the demand by women for equal pay has been constantly blocked by the argument of a man's dependents. A third consequence was that when women entered the labour market they did so under depressed conditions with prejudice against them, and a fourth that the entire standard of health, comfort and amenity in the home depended upon the arbitrary good-will of the male wage-earner.

This complete dependence has been recently modified in various minor ways. Poor-law administration in this country has always considered, however grudgingly, the needs of individuals, not of a phantom family of "mother, father and three children." During the war the immense exodus of bread-winners into the army was facilitated by the payment of maintenance allowances to the wives and children. The rise in the standard of health which followed this surprised even its official recorders. The various war pensions schemes were similarly allotted according to the actual number of dependents, and by the end of the war, society had grown accustomed to the idea of an income allocated according to the needs of individuals.

From 1919 to 1925 certain women's organisations including most of the equalitarian groups, demanded what was not strictly an equalitarian measure—the extension to civilians of the widows' pension system practised in the army. Their argument ran that since most women were withdrawn—by custom or compulsion—from the labour market upon marriage, they and their children were left in a desperate plight if their bread-winner died. It was often impossible to return to skilled employment; the unskilled ranks of charwomen, button-stitchers, office-cleaners and the like were already overcrowded; the children suffered. In 1925 they secured in England a measure of national contributory pensions for widows of insured persons.

But there are other schemes which carry the principle much further. In 1916 a M. Romanet of Grenoble established in his factory a system of allocation of payment according to family needs. In 1921 this was extended to other firms. To-day *"caisses de compensation"* are established all over France where weekly grants, contributed by employers and employed alike, are paid according to the number of each workman's family dependents. In Europe the system has been spreading sporadically in Germany, Belgium, Holland, Austria and Czecho-slovakia. At Geneva the International Labour Organisation has adopted it. In England the London School of Economics and a few other individual associations are experimenting with it.

Opinion about the method is hotly contested. In this country the dignified and authoritative member for the Combined English Universities, Miss Eleanor Rathbone, M.P., has been its most strenuous and effective advocate. But her opponents attack her position from varying angles. One group declares that to pay women simply for being housewives and mothers is to perpetuate their status of domestic tutelage, and their classification with children as dependents. They prefer the system of equal pay, free competition, and a heavier social emphasis upon paternal duty. If fathers as well as mothers practised "parentcraft," they say, the bathing and feeding and shepherding of small children would not fall so heavily upon the mother. They point to the Russian example of free clinics and crèches, communal meals and wage-earning mothers, and find this preferable. The Dutch socialists, when the scheme was advocated for their country, argued that it tended, when practised, to depress wages, and Neo-Malthusians deplore its probable effect upon population, though in actual experience allowances do not seem to have encouraged over-large families.

But so long as the family is as firmly embedded in our social structure as it is to-day, some such redistribution of income has great advantages. For the present system is fair neither to men nor women. The economic legend whereby every man is supposed to support two or three children, and every woman none, has the result of reducing the wages of both. Logically, payment should either be wholly according to merit or wholly according to need; to-day it attempts a compromise which does justice to neither.

So women are not rich, but they are growing richer. They are not secure, but they have recognised the value of security. They have, since their enfranchisement, obtained a slightly larger share of the national income; and some at least are devising methods whereby the division may be more fairly made.

.   .   .   .   .   .

These are generalisations. I have considered the history of the last century-and-a-half in England rather than elsewhere, because the movement for emancipation started here, and has followed much the same lines in most Western European countries, in the British Dominions and in the United States of America. There are local and individual differences which leave a pre-Victorian and a post-war Georgian family living to-day side by side in the same boarding-house at the same moment. And never in the whole world's history, so far as we can tell, has a social movement been without exceptions.

To-day we live in an age of transition. The excitement still aroused by any discussion concerning the merits, status, ambitions, foibles and mistakes of women is in part a nervous excitement arising out of the emotional entanglement which binds the sexes one towards the other; in part it is an historical excitement having its roots deep in the past.

On the very day on which I wrote these paragraphs I attended a public luncheon organised by the enterprising young Miss Christine Foyle to celebrate the Jubilee Celebrations of Dame Ethel Smyth. Sir Thomas Beecham was in the Chair, and he made a remarkable and laudatory speech about Dame Ethel, referring to her as the greatest living woman and the greatest woman composer of all time. No other woman musician, he said, came within a hundred miles of her; and no other, he thought, ever would. He seemed pleased at this, as though it were a tribute to the peculiar genius of the great musician whom he praised. But why was he so sure? And why was he pleased? Why is it still considered a bad joke or a miracle to succeed in one of the spheres hitherto largely occupied by men? Why, in 1934, are women themselves often the first to repudiate the movements of the past hundred and fifty years, which have gained for them at least the foundations of political, economic, educational and moral equality? What is all the fuss about? To answer these questions we shall have to examine more closely certain aspects of our own time and country, regarding them as fairly characteristic examples of the inconveniences of transition from one social status to another.

CHAPTER III

THE INCONVENIENCES OF TRANSITION

The Inferiority Complex

IN the end, what matters is an attitude of mind.
Last year a group of young geological students went
on a scientific expedition across Iceland. As it happened,
the weather was good, fortune favourable, the adventurers
tough, and the journey quite successful. But the party
had certainly risked hardship and not a little danger. On
her return, one of the members, commenting upon the
death of a young airman reported in the press, cried:
"They oughtn't to *do* such things! It's not right to run
such risks." "But it was his job," she was reminded.
"And you of all people oughtn't to object to people
running risks for the sake of your job. What about your
own trip to Iceland, and the expedition across Greenland
you are planning?" "Oh, but that's different," said the
girl. "I'm only a woman."

The story is true. It also seems significant.

That young woman of 1933 was superficially as unlike
her predecessors of a hundred years ago as any girl could
be. Her hair was cropped, her limbs muscular and sturdy,
her hands, brown and coarsened by grubbing about among
rocks and machinery, considerably less well cared for than
her brother's. She could drive and repair a car, find her
way across a continent, take with some distinction her
Science Tripos at Cambridge, discuss with some precision
the problems of the differential calculus, order a luncheon
(including the correct wines) in a first-class restaurant,

97

climb a rock-face, and investigate intelligently its geological strata. She was, moreover, loyal, modest, intelligent and attractive—a highly promising specimen of any generation. And it was characteristic of her generation that her particular expression of sex-inferiority should take the form of seeing no reason why she should not risk her life, but objecting strongly to the same risk by a male contemporary. "I'm only a woman."

In a household I know, where both husband and wife are vigorous feminists, both professional people, and the wife, if anything, a little more successful and certainly richer than the husband, the small son recently, while playing a game, observed, "Now let's address this parcel to Mr. and Mrs. Green—or Mr. Green alone will do, because he's the most important person." Asked why Mr. Green (a wholly imaginary character) should be more important, the child could not say. He just took it for granted that, being a man, he would be.

This deeply rooted inferiority-superiority ratio between girls and boys has more than one explanation.

It is traditional. The picture of the man striding forward to conquer new worlds and the woman following wearily behind, a baby in her arms, is imprinted deeply upon the racial imagination. It colours our half-conscious phrases, our emotions, the very emphasis with which we speak and the tones of our voice. Children learn from these before they can even distinguish the sense of individual words. Boys and girls alike observe from their infancy that the policeman magnificently directing the traffic at the cross-roads is a man; the engine driver is a man; the prime minister, the sweep, the lamplighter and the King (a much more exciting nursery character than the Queen) —all these are men. God is a man. In countries where certain deities also may be female, social legend sees that female divinity does not encourage any human equalitarianism.

Nor is that all. In spite of the provisions of schools and colleges for girls which are, if less well endowed, at least in teaching methods equal to those provided for boys, girls' education is still not, in the vast majority of households, considered as serious an affair as their brothers'. When economies have to be made, it is the girl who usually goes to the less expensive school, the boy who must, at all costs, be given "every chance."

This is not due to sheer perversity; it still hangs to a large extent upon the tradition of the male bread-winner. Parents believe that their boy will grow into a family man, head of a household, provider for female and juvenile dependents; and that the girl may earn a little pocket-money or talk largely about her independence until she marries comfortably and "settles down," prepared to make some good man happy while he in turn provides for her.

But supposing that the girl is not withdrawn from the elementary school at fourteen to "help mind the baby," or sent to a cheap private establishment in the locality while her brother goes on to Winchester or Harrow; supposing that her parents give her, so far as they are able, equal educational advantages, what then?

A hundred subtle influences haunt the schoolgirl or university student. She may be as good at intellectual work as her brother; she may beat him. But she cannot play football or cricket as he can; she cannot row so well; she lacks certain of his larger social freedoms. Fathers often pay willingly their son's wine bills, in order that the lad may learn to carry his drink like a gentleman. I have yet to meet the parent prepared happily to sign a cheque in order that his daughter may learn to carry her drink like a lady. The motor-cycles that snort and thunder down the Iffley Road, the solemn facetiousness of the Oxford Union, the superbly idiotic undergraduate clubs, such as the Bullingdon—these are the reserve of the male undergraduate. The young woman lacks their spacious ritual. She may despise it. She has herself little time or money to waste upon catchwords and ceremonial. The pageant and rubric of club life or Masonry ill accord with the quick decisions and improvisation of the domestic tradition. But all ceremony, from the consecration of an archbishop to the toasting of a football captain, has a way of impressing its uninitiated spectators, and making their unorganised individualism appear flimsy, jejeune and anarchical.

And when the examinations have been passed, and the young man and woman together enter the labour market, what then? It is not merely that in most industries and professions the girl is paid less, does less interesting work and has fewer opportunities for promotion; all those things are generally though not universally true. It is much more that at the top of every—or almost every tree—the girl sees, not an older woman seated, but a man. The young L.R.A.M. seeking her first paid job—usually as a teacher—goes to enjoy herself at the Queen's Hall and hears music by Bach, Beethoven, Brahms or Delius, all men, conducted by a man, played by a male orchestra. There may be a soprano in pink satin; there may be a lady harpist. There may be occasional string players modestly tucked away among their trousered colleagues. The young law student having eaten her last dinner and been called to the bar may frequent the Courts and devil for a senior; but the judges, the King's Counsellors, the Lord Chancellor, the Attorney General, and, as a rule, the senior for whom she devils, are not women, and it is still impossible for many able women even to make a bare living from the Law. The young probationer, scuttling down the long corridors of the hospital; the aspirant to the hotel business counting linen in the basement storerooms; the junior reporter encountering upon the stone stairs of the great newspaper building the Boss of the concern, and the factory hand watching the proprietor of the works drive off to a Board meeting—these leaders, these field-marshals whose baton she does not, she feels, carry in her knapsack, are not women. They are men. "Their women" are their wives, who sometimes venture an elegant appearance in office or factory yard. If the girl is lucky she might meet the genial Dean of the London School of Medicine, or the proprietor of the Honywood Hotels Ltd., or the Managing Director of the National Magazine Company Ltd., or the Vice-Chairman of D. Davis & Sons Ltd., these she would find, surprisingly enough perhaps, to be all of her own sex; but Elizabeth Bolton, Lady Honywood, Miss Alice Head and Viscountess Rhondda are all unusual people. If the modern girl sees them as portents, forerunners of a great multitude, she is safe enough, but if she sees them as isolated and unnatural phenomena, it is improbable that her ambition will sustain her courage.

Men are at the tops of all the trees. And a dozen good reasons exist to convince the girl that this state of affairs is right and natural. Are not men stronger? Her brother could throw a cricket ball further, could run faster; her father can lift heavier weights than her mother; he carries the trunks downstairs; he unscrews the tin she cannot shift. It also often happens that, just as the girl is first facing the complexities and problems of the adult world, her mother is going through the physical and nervous disturbances of the climacteric. With some women this creates little trouble; but it would be stupid to deny that under present conditions the majority of women do, from the ages of about forty-five to fifty, suffer from headaches, indigestion, low blood-pressure or some other form of disabling if not crippling disability. The fact that later most of them regain their second youth, and live to a longer, healthier and more active old age than their husbands, is a truth which their daughters, aware chiefly of the domestic scene below their noses, are tempted to ignore. To most young people in their twenties, middle-aged women all too often appear as physical crocks. And that discourages them.

Another powerful motive for inferiority arises from the military values which—deny them as we will—dominate even our own comparatively pacific nation. In certain other countries, they are not denied at all. It is all very well to maintain, indicating the poignant evidence of *Testament of Youth*, that women in war time suffer equally with men; that recently they have played an active part as Waacs, Wrafs, Wrens, V.A.D.'s, motor drivers, munition workers, or soldiers in the Polish and Russian Women's Army Corps; that the next war will draw no line between combatants and civilians. Our reason affirms these things; emotion, quickened by a flag, a drum, a uniform, speaks otherwise. Pipers playing up the road, the austere dedicated rapture upon a young man's face, the solemn affirmation of a military funeral—these ignite the imagination, and these are masculine moments.

Hero-worship attends the man of action, and for so many generations the man of action *par excellence* has been the soldier. As I write, the most successful music-hall turn in London is that of Miss Cicely Courtneidge, surrounded by a chorus of guardsmen, on the stage of the Victoria Palace, singing, "There's something about a soldier that is fine, fine, fine!" It is a far cry from that frivolity to the superb pageant of the Armistice Day Cenotaph Service, the Trooping of the Colour, or the muffled drums of a military funeral, but their combined effect impresses even those who have intellectually rejected all military sentiment. There are few of us so immune from mass suggestion that we can watch unmoved the unselfconscious dedication and discipline of young men marching. The final sanction of ritual comes from death. That is why the Church and the Army alone have that incomparable power to sway our imaginations. And Church and Army are masculine institutions. The solemn drama of the Mass is a man's drama, performed by men in memory of a Man who was God. The slow procession of a military funeral is a man's procession, performed by men in memory of a man who was a servant of his country.

I hate war. I think military values pernicious. I believe that the world would be healthier if all military pageants were abolished. Yet I cannot hear a band playing in the street, or see the kilts of a Highland regiment swing to the march of men, or watch a general ride to review his regiment, without a lift of the heart and an instinctive homage of the senses. I am an agnostic, and was reared a Protestant. But I cannot see the priest move through the stately motions of the Mass and hear the bell, the Latin words, the organ music, without an emotional response of awe and reverence.

And I am sure that millions of women, stirred by similar feelings, are prepared to adore the dedicated patriotism of soldiers, and think less of themselves for their subordinate mission as spectators or congregation, and, thinking less of themselves, to belittle their own contribution to society. One of the great virtues of the Militant Suffrage movement was its mastery of the art of ritual. Its great processions, its pageants, banners, badges, its prison uniforms, its martyr's funerals, for a brief time took the place usually held by military or religious ceremony in the imagination of those who saw them. In Russia the Workers' Processions and pageants in the Red Square at Moscow are performed by women as well as men; and in Russia more than anywhere perhaps, women are losing their inferiority complex.

For, so long as they belittle their contribution to society, women are apt to leave it to the mercy of every distraction. Throughout long centuries they have been told that a woman's first and only duty is domestic. It is not possible in one or two generations to counteract that long tradition.

The woman doctor, architect or engineer may do her work effectively, but the illness of a relative or a catastrophe in the household arrangements throws a double burden upon her. Husband and wife in a home may both be professional workers; but it is the wife who is expected to order the meals, superintend the nurseries, arrange the entertainments and engage the domestic staff, just as in the case of industrial employees though both may go to the factory and the wife's may be the hardest work, it is she who is expected to prepare the food, clean the house and mend the children's clothes in her so-called leisure. While Carlyle was shutting himself up in his sound-proof room, and sacrificing his wife to his dyspeptic or creative agonies, Mrs. Gaskell was writing her novels at the end of a dining-room table, among a constant whirl of children, servants, draughts and callers. Carlyle's achievement, considered by purely intellectual standards, was the more impressive; but the author of *Mary Barton* and *North and South* had an alert intelligence and imagination which, had they been adequately respected, might have raised her literary work from competence to greatness. Intensity of passion is a constituent part of genius; and it is still true that unless a woman is highly egotistical or highly fortunate, her struggle to obtain freedom from domestic preoccupation exhausts a major part of her energy before it ever finds its way near her work. To be sensitive, to be public spirited, to have imaginative insight into the needs of others, are qualities which should increase the value of any artist or administrator; often, if she happens to be a woman, they merely impose upon her personal obligations which, in a better-organised society, could be acquitted otherwise and by other, differently qualified people.

But this tendency to consider everybody else's interests more important than their own is one of the major expressions of women's inferiority complex. If they dared to believe in their own capacity, if they had learned that the price to be paid for achievement is not merely the sacrifice of oneself, but often the sacrifice of others, their achievements would appear less mediocre. When a woman believes enough in her own mission to be ruthless —a Mrs. Siddons, a Florence Nightingale, a Mrs. Pankhurst—then, indeed, something happens. But most women dread before everything to "cause an upset" or inconvenience a family; and their work suffers.

I believe that this is one of the most formidable handicaps confronting women; but every outstanding achievement by a woman decreases it. When an Amy Johnson breaks aviation records, when a Madame Curie discovers radium, an Ethel Smyth composes a Mass, a Frances Perkin controls perhaps the most difficult government department in the American New Deal—then it becomes a trifle harder for young girls to tell themselves: "It doesn't matter. I'm only a woman." The possibility of achievement has been vindicated.

The Chivalry Complex

The inferiority complex is recognisable, vulnerable and direct. The chivalry complex attacks us in far subtler ways.

The masculine version rests upon Mr. G. K. Chesterton's theory that women are "uncrowned queens," so much purer, nobler, finer and more sensitive than men that they should never be allowed to soil their white hands in the world's dirty work. During the fight for the vote women heard appeals to "Ministering Angels," to "Civilising Influence," and "gentler natures" until they were sick of them. In the name of Noble Maternity they were asked to tolerate a legal system by which a mother was not the guardian of her own legitimate child; in the name of Purity they were asked to turn a blind eye to the White Slave traffic, the Contagious Diseases Acts, and the outlawry of Prostitutes harried by a corrupting penal code. In the name of Gentleness they were invited to raise no finger against a social system which allowed children to be assaulted, neglected or starved.

That attitude still persists. It is often combined with an artificial and sentimentalised respect for motherhood. It is cultivated by the social tradition of Catholic Christianity and colours the papal encyclicals on social subjects. Frequently it is combined with an exaggerated idea of women's physical fragility. In January 1934 Mr. A. J. Cummings aroused a vehement controversy in the *News-Chronicle* by writing a lively attack upon the young men of the day. Are they flabby? he asked, and replied in the affirmative. A typical answer was from one correspondent who accepted the accusation but attributed the blame to the young women. These, he said, had grown so muscular and independent that men no longer felt called upon to protect them, so had lost the natural motive for keeping fit and keen.

Set down in its crude form, the argument is comical and characteristic. But it goes deep, it dies hard, and few influences have caused more unhappiness in this period of transition.

For in part, of course, it is a noble concept. The footsore builder's labourer who drags himself upright in a crowded tube to offer his seat to the girl typist is moved by the same impulse which led neolithic man to guard the mouth of the cave when his woman suckled her child. The motive is identical. Muscular unburdened man uses his strength to protect the woman made vulnerable and dependent through the obligations of maternity. But the urban conditions of the twentieth century have changed a once admirable and socially useful impulse into a superstition destructive of human happiness. For in the tube the builder's labourer is probably already over-tired; he should be sitting to rest his varicose veins. The typist has probably sat for eight hours or more at her machine; the motions of strap-hanging would be beneficial to her arms, legs and liver. But by social tradition all women (however virginal, muscular and tough) are potentially pregnant; all men, however, physically unfit and tired, are muscular heroes; and the strong must at all costs protect the weak. The strap-hanging incident is merely one minor absurdity of the chivalry complex. It has other and far more serious social aspects.

In 1934 for reasons I have tried to explain in the previous chapter, women find jobs more easily than men; they are cheaper, they are less well organised; their numbers in industry and the professions are constantly diminished by the drain of marriage and domestic obligation. Therefore to-day one frequently encounters a new social pheno-menon—the successful earning woman supporting the unemployed man. He may be a husband, father, brother, friend or lover; he may be an employee or former col-league. He may simply be a casual acquaintance. But the effect is almost invariably painful.

There have been rich women and poor men before. The story of the impecunious youth who successfully woos and wins the great heiress is as old as the fairy tale of "The Princess and the Swineherd." But those heiresses were merely the stamp on the cheque handing over their father's fortune. Tom Jones might seem to accept money from his wife; he knew, and she knew and society knew that he was really taking it from her father, and convention has never objected to man's accepting money from his father-in-law.

But from a woman, he loathes it. The integrity of his honour is violated. The Count d'Orsay may have per-mitted Lady Blessington to write her fingers to the bone to pay his debts; ostensibly the money was always his and he was going to make a fortune. Some husbands were content in the early days of the Industrial Revolution, to live on their wives' earnings; but at least the earnings then were legally theirs, and they thought no more of it than the Nyassaland chief who dozes in the sun while his wives carry water, grind the corn and cure the skins for him. These are exceptions.

To-day it is a common enough experience in a restaurant to hear a young man and woman quarrelling over who shall pay for lunch. "I've not fallen so low as to let a woman pay my bill for me," he grumbles, scowling. She, aware that she is earning three, four or more pounds a week, while he perhaps is an unemployed remittance man living with his parents who allow him a weekly pound for pocket money, finally lets him pay in order not to wound his pride; but she takes care not to put herself in that position again. Their friendship crumbles. Her chivalry meets his, and common sense is overridden.

But their dilemma is negligible compared with the predicament of the professional or business woman in love with a man poorer than herself. There are men who will not even kiss a girl in a taxi for which they have not paid. There are to-day, men and women fitted by every other circumstance of character and temperament to marry each other, prevented only by the tradition that the husband supports the wife. In some cases they know well enough that if she marries she will lose her work; in others his chivalry complex forbids the man to let his wife pay the housekeeping bills. "I will not be your gigolo," cries the lover, desperate between prejudice and passion. And the woman, aware of her expensive training, of the obligation which she owes, perhaps, to individuals and institutions who have made it possible, aware of the possibilities of usefulness which lie before her, weighs these against the doubtful chance of making one man happy on an income already inadequate for his needs alone—and the marriage does not take place.

If social and traditional pressure were removed, the difficulty would disappear. Marriage—the private contract of love and fidelity between two individuals—is a personal matter concerning them alone. Differences of means should not affect it. The setting up of a family is a more social affair and has economic problems; but, apart from prejudice, there is no reason why a wife as well as a widow should not earn for her children, provided that society should not, as it does at present, throw one obstacle after another in the path of the wage-earning mother.

But the chivalry complex not only violates common sense; it panders to laziness. After all, the great majority of people in this world are not eager, ambitious, conscientious, talented, taut with desire to give to society more than they get from it; most people are willing enough to lie back upon any situation which will provide a comfortable resting place. Women like being "taken care of" and "protected" as much as men. As much—no more. The most prominent masculine characteristic is happily not an appetite for a "cushy job and no trouble"; the most prominent feminine characteristic is not a desire for "some good man to look after her." But there is this distinction; under the chivalry complex between men and women, it is still regarded as a virtue in a man to "look after" his wife and daughters; further, it is still regarded as a virtue in a woman to submit gracefully to his protection. Dependence, slightly shameful in a man, is, under this tradition, pleasing in a woman. To-day any clever woman, even in business or a profession, learns how to turn on the you're-a-great-big-strong-man-and-I'm-a-poor-little-weak-helpless-woman-do-look-after-me manner. If she does not, she is damned as domineering and uncivil; and the final insult to a woman is to accuse her of domination.

This being so, there is every psychological temptation for a woman to allow herself to be "protected and provided for." It is not always pleasant to spring out of bed when the alarm clock announces half-past seven, to dress hurriedly, to catch a train into the city, to submit to day-long imprisonment in factory, shop, office, or consulting-room, to conciliate clients, to soothe superiors, to disentangle the complicated grievances, stupidities and susceptibilities of subordinates. The vision of leisure, liberty and irresponsibility which sometimes appears to be the lot of the well-to-do married woman, ensnares the weary or the unadventurous. To lie still in the big double bedroom and to struggle no more for contracts or commissions; to eat meals for which somebody else has willingly paid, to buy clothes unearned by desperate battles against the shyness or fatigue, or the slow-working or inflexible brain that handicaps one's professional movements, to be free to play golf on a Tuesday afternoon, or to take the children out picnicking on a Thursday morning, all these pleasures of leisured matrimony militate against any universal desire on the part of women to remain economically independent after marriage.

And when this surrender is not only pleasant but popular, when it is the only attitude quite satisfactory to the husband's pride, then indeed chivalry weights the scales. And then indeed the man unable to "keep" his wife is further embittered. He is shamed by a breach of tradition. He is shamed by the thought that his wife secretly despises him, that whatever her protests of preference and enjoyment, she would really like to resign her job and come home and be supported by him. He blames himself and blames society and blames her, perhaps, most of all. And then we are told that "these independent women do not make a success of marriage."

Until a new chivalry of equal and independent beings, one towards the other, is developed, this complex will continue to trouble the relationships between men and women of the modern world.

The Slump Complex

These disadvantages are further accentuated by a group of reactions which I shall call the "slump complex." They have been particularly conspicuous during the past five years, and affect especially those young men and women who grew into maturity since the Armistice. Their condition is natural; it is directly attributable to the circumstances of their epoch, but they are apt to overlook this and mistake it for an unalterable law of nature ignored with naïve ignorance by their elders.

The effect of the slump upon women's economic position is most obvious, not only in the problems of unemployment among both industrial and professional women, but still more in the bitterness surrounding the question of married women's paid employment, "pin money" office girls, unorganised casual female factory labour, and claims to alimony, maintenance and separation allowances. These are the dilemmas of scarcity. It is here that the shoe pinches when national purchasing power has failed to distribute adequately the products of industry.

During the War, women entered almost every branch of industry and most of the professions. Even the Diplomatic Service, still, when this book is written, closed to women (though a committee is inquiring into future possibilities) was temporarily invaded by the adventurous Getrude Bell who, under the modest title of Temporary Assistant Political Officer, really acted as British representative in Iraq. In transport, engineering, chemicals, textiles, tailoring and woodwork, women took the places which, ever since the sorting-out process which followed the first disorganised scramble of the Industrial Revolution, had been reserved to men. They took and they enjoyed them.

Then the men returned, and on demobilisation demanded again the jobs which they had left. The position was not simple.

Some of the men had received promises that their work should be kept for them; but of these, some did not return. Some women surrendered their shovels, lathes and hoes without a grievance. Their work had been "for the duration of the war" and they had no desire to retain it.

But others thought differently. Women, they told themselves, had been excluded from the more highly-skilled and better-paid industrial posts for two or more generations. They had been told that certain processes were beyond their power. It was a lie. During the war they had proved it to be so, by their own skill and efficiency. Why surrender without a word opportunities closed to them by fraud and falsehood? They had as much right to wheel, loom or cash-register as any man. Why then pretend that they were intruders in a world which was as much their own as their brothers'?

Some of these malcontents were nevertheless driven out; some stayed because their employers found them cheaper, and became unwilling blacklegs. One notable example of this was the case of "writing assistants" in the Civil Service, the lowest-graded category of clerks, engaged on purely mechanical and routine tasks. Organisations of ex-service men repeatedly petitioned that men should be admitted to this work; but the refusal was justified on the grounds that the work—besides being inadequately paid—was "too mechanical" for men.

The boom came; the new industries of the South sprang up like mushrooms; cities grew. For six or seven years it seemed as though production was infinite in expansion and the presence of women at unfamiliar tasks, though arousing occasional local criticism, not nationally disturbing.

The slump changed all that. After 1928, jobs became not duties which war-time propaganda taught girls that it was patriotic to perform, but privileges to be reserved for potential bread-winners and fathers of families. Women were commanded to go back to the home.

The bitterness began which has lasted ever since—the women keeping jobs and the men resenting it—the men regaining the jobs and the women resenting it.

On November 14th, 1933, the Central Hall, Westminster, was crowded for a mass meeting of women's organisations to proclaim the right of married women to paid employment. The crowds, the banners, the enthusiasm, echoed, faintly but unmistakably the spirit of pre-war suffrage meetings. The following March the Hall was nearly filled again when a similar demand was made for "Equal Pay for Equal Work."

In January 1934 the *News-Chronicle* published an article on Women Secretaries by a well-known writer, pleading the advantages of higher payment in order that the girls might not only be better fed and housed, but neater in appearance, more self-respecting and therefore more efficient. On the next day a correspondent had written in to the paper, bitterly complaining: "Better pay and smarter clothes for women: unemployment and patched pants for men."

The men have a real grievance. So long as women are content to accept lower wages, to remain unorganised, and to regard wage-earning as a "meanwhile" occupation till marriage, their cheap labour will continue to blackleg; and during any widespread contraction of trade, under a system of competitive capitalism, employers will deliberately use them for this purpose.

But the trouble is complex. The slump did not only depress the economic life of the country; it depressed its political, its intellectual and spiritual life.

Just after the war, society was infected by a rush of idealism to the head. Democracy and reason, equality and co-operation were acclaimed as uncontested virtues. In the new constitutions of Europe and America were incorporated splendid statements about the freedom of opinion, equality of the sexes, accessibility of education. We were about to build a brave new world upon the ruins of catastrophe.

The children who to-day are young men and women were assured at school of a good time coming. Everything evil was the result of four years' war; that horror had passed; they were to inherit the benefits purchased by sacrifice. Old hampering conventions had broken down; superstitions were destroyed; the young had come into their kingdom.

It was under the influence of this optimism that young women cherished ambitions for the wider exercise of their individual powers, and saw no limit to the kind and quality of service which they might offer to the community.

About 1926, after the General Strike in England and its failure, after the entry of Germany into the League of Nations and the delay by the Powers in making good their promises, the slump in idealism began to set in. Reason, democracy, the effort of the individual human will, liberty and equality were at a discount. As economic opportunities shrank, so the hopefulness and idealism of the early post-war period dwindled.

In Italy, Germany and Ireland a new dream of natural instinctive racial unity was arising, which designed for women a return to their "natural" functions of housekeeping and child-bearing; while in the English-speaking countries a new anti-rational philosophy combined with economic fatalism, militated against the ebullient hopes which an earlier generation had pinned to education, effort, and individual enterprise.

All generalisations are false. In every civilised country are little groups of older women with memories of suffrage struggles, and young women who grew up into the post-war optimism, and whose ideas remain unchanged by the fashions of the hour. It is they who still organise protests against reaction; who in national and international societies defend the political, civil and economic equality of men and women; who invade new territories of achievement; who look towards a time when there shall be no wrangling over rights and wrongs, man's place and woman's place, but an equal and co-operative partnership, the individual going unfettered to the work for which he is best suited, responsibilities and obligations shared alike.

But these groups of professional women, organisers, artists, writers, members of societies like the Equal Rights International, the Open Door Council, the National Women's Party of America, the Women's International League of Peace and Freedom, are now in a minority and they know it.

The younger women more closely resemble a description recently given of the newly-adult generation in modern France. "They are fatalists. They are sensible. They are not interested in ideas. They believe that a war is coming against Germany which will destroy all individual plans, and they say 'Que Faire?' They do not choose their work. They have to take what they can get and be glad of that. They marry early, feeling that life being so short and uncertain they must make sure of posterity while they can. They are completely indifferent to large general principles or long-distance hopes of social amelioration. They have stoical courage but no enterprise, no hope, and no idealism. They ask for discipline, not freedom; for security, not for opportunity. Many of them are returning to orthodox religion; but few of them seem to have experienced religious ardour."

One man I know, an ex-minister of the Crown in this country, gave an explanation that the young generation just recently adult has grown up in a time of huge impersonal events—the War, the Boom, the Slump. News

is reported daily of immense catastrophes over which
they can have no control, the Japanese and Indian earth-
quakes, Chinese famine, African drought. The cheap
daily press and wireless bring these facts vividly home to
them in a way their ancestors never knew. The individual
will seems unimportant, the individual personality is
dwarfed, by happenings on so large a scale. The world is
too much for them. They give it up, content to be
passive passengers in a vehicle which they cannot steer.

This is the slump complex—this narrowing of ambition,
this closing-in alike of ideas and opportunities. Somewhere, a spring of vitality and hope has failed. As though
it required too great an effort against such odds to assume
responsibility for their own individual destiny, they fall
back upon tradition, instinct, orthodoxy. The slump is
really a general resignation by humanity of its burden of
initiative, and women fall under its influence as much
as men.

The Modern Girl

In 1934 the subject of the modern girl is as lively as
it was in 1428 when St. Bernardino of Siena preached a
sermon which sounds curiously like almost any letter to
the *Daily Express* signed "Mother of Seven" or "Indignant."
"O women," cried the saint, "when I see you with those
sleeves of yours, and some there are that have altered them
by splitting them from end to end so that the arm shows
through. Why don't you go naked? Oh, oh, oh, oh,
the shamelessness of women! Will nothing make you
blush? Is there never a harlot you have seen with new
clothes but you did not run to copy her fashions? Why
do you copy her unless you wish to appear as a harlot
yourself?"

To-day in most civilised countries similar accusations
may be heard. The conventional ideas about the young
modern woman suggest that she is:

(i) Rude to her parents and seniors and impatient of authority;

(ii) Neglectful of her real duties;

(iii) Selfish about her pleasures;

(iv) Unconcerned about matters of public interest;

(v) Uncontrolled in habits, given to drinking, smoking and sexual promiscuity.

Apparently the same conventional ideas have been held in every age, so there is nothing remarkable in that. But certain phenomena perhaps are characteristic of this present time.

This is, as Miss Cicely Hamilton has observed in her amusing *Little Arthur's History of the Twentieth Century*, the Age of the Child; during the past twenty years children in Europe and America have been considered, propitiated, indulged and studied as perhaps they never had been before. One result of this is that they are not afraid of their parents. Their timid reverence offered to adults has disappeared. Mothers and daughters discuss their family problems on equal terms. This is a different thing from disrespect for authority. The cry of the youth movements of to-day, in Germany, Russia, Ireland and elsewhere, for Leadership and for Discipline, offers evidence of a taste for subordination that is all too eager.

But in the industrial areas, especially those most affected by the slump, a new element has entered into the relationship between parents and children. As it is often easier for women than for men to find employment, so it is easier for adolescents than for adults. It therefore often happens that young girls are working in factories, private domestic service, shops and laundries, and using their small wage to support their parents. In England under the Means Test principle of unemployment insurance, this support is not voluntary but compulsory. The parents' benefit is adjusted according to the children's earnings. In the spring of 1934 a leather-curer of Birmingham killed himself because he could not endure dependence upon his children. In the days of the Old Testament, Hebrew patriarchs regarded their families as potential wealth. Tribal chiefs in Africa do the same to-day. But these twentieth-century parents have been brought up on a creed of consideration for their children which makes their involuntary dependence doubly hard. And sometimes, no doubt, the children show resentment. It is not always easy, even for generous and exploitable adolescence, to shoulder the adult burden of responsibility.

The second accusation is that modern girls neglect their real duty. The answer here depends upon a definition. What is their duty? To be human beings, claiming all labour as their province, seeking full exercise for their individual abilities—or to be "womanly women" according to the newest of the fashions?

Much sociological information can be gained from the modern craft of advertisement-copy-writing. The catalogue published by Messrs. Harrods of Knightsbridge for January 1934 contains a "Fashion Forecast" which opens thus:

"Women are going to be their normal feminine selves in 1934. Parisian dressmakers have decided in favour of a sweetly feminine silhouette for the coming spring which will accentuate a woman's charm by means of ruffles, frills and other delightful artifices. Square shoulders, with their angular effects, will give way to soft fullness lower in the arm. Even evening gowns, boasting bare shoulders, will have a suggestion of sleeves or a deep frill beneath which the arms will be discreetly covered in quite a prudish manner."

The psychology of clothes is not unimportant. Nowadays, thanks to the true democracy of the talkies, twopenny fashion journals and inexpensive stores, it is possible for one fashion to affect a whole hemisphere with no distinction of class and little of pocket. The girls advised to acquire "sweetly feminine silhouettes" are not confined to one group of rich young debutantes. The post-war fashion for short skirts, bare knees, straight, simple chemise-like dresses, shorts and pyjamas for sports and summer wear, cropped hair and serviceable shoes is waging a defensive war against this powerful movement to reclothe the female form in swathing trails and frills and flounces, to emphasise the difference between men and women—to recall Woman, in short, to Her True Duty—of what?

Theoretically the bearing of sons and recreation of the tired warrior. Actually it is a vexed question whether the swathed and corseted lady bears sons as well as the athletic lithe young woman with well-developed muscles. The high infant mortality rate of the most corseted era would suggest that flounces and wasp-waists, as an aid to maternity, are over-rated.

The girl of 1934 torn between conflicting definitions of her duty, oppressed by the three emotional complications that I mentioned—the inferiority, chivalry and slump complexes—undoubtedly finds this a hard and puzzling world, and her true duty as illusive as the solution to most other moral problems.

That she is selfish about her own pleasures is another accusation which cannot be answered by a simple affirmation or denial. "Pleasures" to-day are more conspicuous because more commercialised than they used to be. The cinema, dance-hall, public tennis-court and swimming-bath, the silent swoop of cycling clubs in close-locked flight down the country roads—these social phenomena are obvious. Anyone can stroll through the suburbs of a provincial town and see girls in their light frocks playing tennis; anyone can see, in the parks and squares of modern industrial cities, the young people from factories and squalid streets, running in shorts and socks round the ash track, playing feeble but merry tennis on the red rubble courts, lounging on the edge of the bathing-pools. "In *my* day," say the critics, thinking of the past century, "those girls would have been sitting at home and sewing —or polishing the silver—or minding the new baby." They forget that modern taste hardly approves of the heterogeneous exhibitions of embroidery—mute witnesses of lifetimes sacrificed to the moloch of Domestic Occupation—which once adorned each self-respecting parlour. They forget that modern medical science disapproves of the sedentary habit suggested by such tributes, that modern education "finds something better to do" for its graduates; just as in spite of their fantastic clumsiness and archaism modern houses are no longer arranged so that their care will occupy as many instead of as few hours as possible, and that modern families are not of a size which will keep married women perpetually occupied by tending the latest baby. For better or worse, we have to-day more leisure, and young women spending their free time in the open air are more conspicuous than their cloistered ancestors. The measure of their selfishness or unselfishness seems to be an individual matter.

The accusation that modern girls are unconcerned with matters of public interest is harder to disprove. The majority of all people are unconcerned with matters of public interest—men and women, young and old alike. Owing to the political habit of camouflage it is not possible to ascertain the precise proportion, for instance, of active women members of under thirty in the political parties. It is true that young industrial women are harder to organise than young men in trades unions; but the reasons here are not wholly attributable to the natural frivolity of the female nature. Young girls have more domestic obligations than young men, which make attendance at meetings and committees more difficult. Their wages are lower, their work less skilled, and most of them expect to leave either voluntarily or involuntarily, their jobs on marriage. Where this last condition is not the rule—as in the textile trades—women are far more keen on their trades union membership; while among the more highly skilled workers, women doctors and women teachers are as much interested as their male colleagues in professional organisation.

A recent census of conversation was taken in an English sweet factory to ascertain what the young girls talked about when performing their mechanical and monotonous business. Cinema stars, men friends and private gossip came out at the top of the schedule. Had the census been taken among men, sport (including football, dog racing and horse racing) would probably have taken the place of the cinema, then women, and then private gossip. When lives are restricted, the routine of work and leisure unvaried, limited and dull, it is not surprising that the vivid emotional romance of the Screen, or the swift, hopeful hazards of gambling should capture imagination. Hunger and love, the two basic desires, chain the hearts of men to a perpetual desire for wealth which satisfies hunger and buys them love, and of women to a perpetual desire for love which secures—they hope—wealth enough to satisfy hunger.

As for politics, art, social service, religion and other impersonal interests, these have always been the taste of a minority. To-day, those circumstances which result in the slump complex combine to make that minority smaller than ever. Young men and women alike feel their individual wills overwhelmed by the huge force of world-wide cataclysms. Young women, then, are not much interested in the valuation of the dollar, the future of democracy, or the exploration of the stratosphere. Neither are young men. But young women are affected by a discouragement which does not afflict their brothers. From childhood upward they hear the cry that "Men hate a clever woman." Baby-faced blondes, the Jean Harlows and Clara Bows of film-fame, are the models of those whom gentlemen prefer. To show intelligence about the organisation of craft guilds, the Marxian theory of profit, or the gold standard, is not only dull but dangerous. It may rob a girl, custom hints, of her attraction for men. In spite of the evidence of successful marriages by intelligent and actively public-spirited women, theory still dictates the ascendancy of the Beautiful but Dumb.

And that brings us to the final criticism: that modern girls are sexually promiscuous, undisciplined and self-indulgent. And here generalisations are far harder to maintain.

Judge Ben Lindsey, for over twenty-six years associated with the Juvenile and Family Court of Denver, Colorado, published in 1928 a book which caused considerable perturbation on both sides of the Atlantic. He called it: *The Revolt of Modern Youth.* He maintained that a social revolution was taking place. Youth, he said, had blown the trumpets of knowledge, and the walls of Jericho were falling down—walls built by conventional tradition, family confidence and innocent youth. During the year 1920-21, he said, his court dealt with 769 girl delinquents of high-school age. "The only reason why the number was not very much larger," he declared, "was that it was physically impossible for me and my very small staff to follow the thing up case by case. For let me repeat here what I have already said, that starting with one case I can uncover a thousand." According to his estimate, one American girl in every ten between the ages of fourteen to seventeen has experienced "sex delinquency," and between the ages of seventeen and twenty-one the percentage is much higher. In later years, the divorce statistics of Denver indicate a failure of 49.5 per cent. of marriages. As for New York: "There are at least 50,000 girls in New York living with men who are not their husbands," said the Judge.

The distress caused by the publication of the book illustrated, among other things, the rarity of that type of conviction expressed by a modern English mother of my acquaintance, who earnestly defined one prime object of education as being to teach young people "to sleep together beautifully." The high estimation set by the Roman Vergilius on his daughter's virginity, so that he preferred to kill her rather than permit her to risk its loss, would to-day certainly be considered exaggerated. But how many daughters in Western Europe of 1934 would willingly tell their fathers that they had become the mistresses of men whom they did not intend to marry?

Statistics are unobtainable. Everyone speaks from his or her own experience. I can only speak of mine and leave it at that. In the middle-class boarding-school which I attended for seven years until 1916, I am unaware that a single girl—and we stayed until the age of 18—had experienced physical intimacy with a man, though some of us had been in love, and one friend of mine at least was engaged. I do not know that one of my contemporaries—and we talked pretty freely—knew the precise nature of Lesbianism.

After 1922 I taught for a number of years in both day- and boarding-schools round London. Of the day-schools I cannot speak. The private lives of the girls were less well known to us. At the boarding-schools, I remember one case only where it became actually known to the staff that a pupil had been intimate with men. In my college days, I do not know for certain that one of my contemporaries had been a man's mistress, though several were or had been engaged to marry. I know of one instance only where a student was suspected of Lesbian practices, but nothing was proved, and the bulk of the students appeared quite ignorant of the supposed nature of her peculiarity. I spent a year in Queen Mary's Army Auxiliary Corps. The girls were recruited from every type of young women in England, including some of the roughest and least reputable. The "Waacs" at one time had a bad name for morals. Few inquiries could be made about respectability, and those that were made would evoke little certainty of answer. At one depôt accommodating over a thousand girls, I knew for certain of one case of pregnancy; at the small camp in France where I spent my longest consecutive period, about nine months, one girl was sent home pregnant; another became the centre of camp gossip, though she swore (and had no reason for lying) that nothing beyond kissing had occurred. I knew intimately about twenty of the fifty-two girls resident there—girls drawn from North of England factories, post offices, and domestic service; we talked with considerable latitude. All the girls picked up temporary "boys" among the English or Australian Tommies in neighbouring camps. All walked, played, danced and flirted with them. It was my duty after the Armistice, as hostel forewoman, to accompany the parties allowed to attend dances organised by the soldiers in recreation huts or French school-rooms hired for the purpose. We used to drive off in lorries or mule-wagons, an escort for each girl. As a matter of course, lights were extinguished, men put their arms round our waists, and thus rode with us—a practice that I, brought up in extremely respectable middle-class surroundings, at first found embarrassing. But I soon grew to enjoy it as well as any one; to recognise the cuddling on the outward journey and the kissing on the homeward one, as courtesies of a society to which it seemed quite natural. I never witnessed conduct which struck my unsophisticated eyes as unseemly. Drunkenness (except for one middle-aged Liverpool docker's wife—a war widow of over forty) was unknown among the girls in our particular camp, and sternly suppressed, by their own code of manners, among the men who came to visit us. I may have been unusually naive; our camp may have been exceptional—I think that in many ways it was; but I have met and talked freely with some of its members since, and we do not know for certain that any girl, with the exception of the spectacled and unattractive nit-wit, ineptly known as "Fluff," sent home discharged to have her baby, who, while in our unit during 1918 and 1919, took a lover.

On the other hand, in the North of England villages which I know well, many betrothed couples follow the old country custom of marrying only after pregnancy. In the towns where youth is more sophisticated and contraception practised, it is harder to obtain a general impression. I know the habits of a small intellectual circle in London, where virginity outside marriage and monogamy within it are apparently exceptional rather than the rule. I know to some extent the provincial towns, where morals vary as widely as incomes and tastes. I know the "rescue work" done by Salvation Army, Church Army and other social workers, among both working-class and middle-class girls. But I still cannot form any clear impression of how far, how frequently, and with what clear mandate of conscience the "modern girl" is sexually promiscuous. ⋅ I read the books; I observe the exceptions to whom accidental misfortune brings publicity; but I do not know—and I do not believe that anybody knows—the exact state of affairs.

Are Spinsters Frustrated?

O. Henry once wrote a short story in which the foreign correspondents of an American paper wanted to cable secret news in a code easily recognisable by their editorial office. So they constructed their sentences from journalistic clichés, knowing that "great white" would suggest "way" as "frustrated" must inevitably suggest "spinster." The two words fit like an egg and egg-cup—and not only west of the Atlantic. The legend of the Frustrated Spinster is one of the most formidable social influences of the modern world.

There is probably no evil under the sun more misery-provoking than frustration. Never to be used to the full scope of our ability, never to serve life's purpose, never to know the rapture of achievement and fulfilment, never to lie back upon the perfect security of completion, aware that, no matter what the future brings, we have had our hour—this is to be deprived of the full stature, the sweetness and significance of human life.

It appears that there are certain experiences which we must enjoy if we are to feel satisfaction. We are unique individuals yet members of a community; a gulf divides us from our fellows, yet we cannot do without them. We need intimacy; we need tenderness; we need love.

But tenderness is not enough. We must have passion. We must at least once in life have burned to the white heat of ecstacy.

We must have achievement. We must feel the pleasure of creation. We are made sufficiently like the image of the God of *Genesis* that we require to build a world for our satisfaction, to rest on the seventh day and know that it is good.

And we need devotion. Whatever spark of divine discontent has been lit within us, we can know no ultimate peace unless we have worshipped some purpose larger than ourselves—a God, a cause, a leader, an idea, even another human person. Without that reverence we walk crippled, our human stature maimed. We are frustrated.

In a world where man still is separated by only a few brief thousand years from the animals whose mortality he inherits, it is natural that he should first look for satisfaction in those experiences which he has shared with them—seeking intimacy in physical contact; ecstasy in that passion's consummation; creative achievement in the reproduction of children, and devotion in personal service to those whom he loves.

In primitive societies, these direct and simple forms of life suffice. Bound upon the turning wheel of the seasons, men and women find in their contact with the land and with each other adequate occupation for their minds and bodies. A minority will always look elsewhere—the artists, the heretics, the restless seekers of passion beyond sexual encounter and achievement beyond the breeding of the race. They have appetites unsatisfied by their neighbours' pleasures; they seek power or beauty or worship or mastery of spirit in activities which may be quite compatible with normal biological developments, but which are not bounded by them. Physically fulfilled, they may be spiritually unsatisfied. In circumstances which may be all that their neighbours demand, they feel frustrated.

Now the identification of this frustration with virginity (for it is commonly though erroneously presumed that all spinsters are virgins) is a comparatively modern notion. In polygamous communities unmated women are so exceptional that they are venerated as priestesses or feared as warlocks. Pagan African witches and Mahometan Sufi mystics alike withdraw from the world of human values into a region of spiritual experience where virginity is respected as possessing a power denied to ordinary flesh and blood. The priestesses of Egypt, the vestals of Rome, the Catholic sisterhoods were set apart from the community. Their state did not inspire pity; it might be feared, disliked or respected; but it was recognised as something positive— a vocation, not a failure, a chosen peculiarity, not a lack of natural fulfilment.

The association of virginity with frustration entered with the Protestant reformation—an odd paradox of Puritanism. The abolition of the monasteries robbed unmarried women of the institution where they had found their special privilege and opportunity. The individualism of Protestant philosophy imposed upon them the obligation of achieving personal success. The same odd materialism which could identify masculine virtue with money-making, identified feminine virtue with husband-getting. Catholics who could call themselves Brides of Christ had no cause for shame, but Protestants who had been unable to win congratulation as brides of men were called "old maids" and foredoomed by folk-lore to "lead an ape in Hell."

In an age where women were almost entirely relegated to domestic activity, except in the lower ranks of labour where they spun, wove, cured leather, dyed, or made lace in their own homes, the unmarried girl was inevitably "odd man out." Independence being almost unheard of, she had to live in some other woman's house, and to remain subject to the will of mother, aunt or sister. She might, as a spinster, really spin, earning her bread by honest industry; yet her place in society was not determined by economic solvency but by social status, and her status had no recognisable value. If she were cultured, she might become governess to other women's children, housekeeper in other ladies' houses, seamstress of other people's finery. She might experience individual tranquillity and fulfilment. A Protestant, Mary Astell, a Harriet Martineau or Florence Nightingale might achieve mastery of a field of work, fame, and their satisfactions. Or she might, seeking illicitly for pleasures lawfully denied her, join the tragic fellowship of witches. A bride of Christ she might not be; but she could be a consort of the devil. She could impose her power with charms and symbols upon the neighbours who despised her. She could risk the hideous torments of ordeal by water and death by burning, in order to enjoy those rarely acknowledged necessities of human happiness—ecstasy, power and devotion—which for most of her companions were provided by their matrimonial experience.

The woman's movement of the past hundred and fifty years has improved the social and economic status of the spinster, and, in some still limited circles, removed her moral obligation of virginity. Teachers, doctors, political organisers, artists and explorers may deliberately choose to remain unmarried in order not to be hampered in their work. In some cases this means that they remain celibate; since the spread of contraceptive knowledge, it generally means that they avoid motherhood. But it is impossible, with any regard for the meaning of words whatsoever, to call such women frustrated; most of them live lives as full, satisfied and happy as any human lives can be. Ecstasy, power and devotion have enriched them; they have served a cause greater than their own personal advantage. They have contributed something to the world and known the satisfaction of creative achievement. It becomes a matter of secondary importance whether they have also experienced the enchanting flattery and relief of being loved; the exquisite intimacy of physical contact, and the extension of personality which parenthood brings with it.

There are hideously frustrated lives to-day. Industrial workers in urban areas repeating monotonous tasks, eating tasteless and inadequate meals, and coming home worn out to crowded and insanitary houses, clamorous with undernourished and undisciplined children, to wives prematurely aged and ugly with child-bearing and fatigue—these are frustrated in their needs for power, beauty, worship, and achievement. The unemployed suffer even more profoundly.

There are the unoccupied women of the middle classes, some married, more unmarried, whose lives have been deliberately designed for an unfulfilled social ideal. They were educated, trained and "brought out" to attract husbands and become mothers of children. For this end, their interests were limited to personal concerns, and carefully detached from permanent absorbtion in activities which might distract their minds from the main purpose. They may "do the flowers," "run the Girl Guides," sit on the committee of the local tennis club, enjoy a season's Winter Sports in Switzerland. But year by year, as these occupations fail to produce their required result—(the husband never materializes, or, having come, he goes)—the routine of "pleasure" or "home life" becomes increasingly exasperating. Nothing has been achieved; no purpose served; the bridge cards are shuffled and re-dealt; the tennis balls brought out or put away; the dance tunes change, but no new partners come. The sum of experience is negation, disappointment and monotony, frequently ending in invalidism, bitterness or neurasthenia.

The elegant ladies, wandering aimlessly from one pleasure resort to another, one luxury hotel to another, finding Antibes as dull as Cowes, baccarat as dull as roulette, Jules as dull as Stephen, heroin as dull as absinthe, and Lesbianism as dull as maternity, are frustrated in their needs for ecstasy, power and devotion. Nursing-homes and sanatoria are filled with neurotics who have worn themselves out vainly seeking physical cures for a spiritual disease.

Why then do we associate spinsterhood with frustration? Bachelors are not presumed to be frustrated. Rather they are regarded as lucky dogs evading their responsibilities, and in countries like Italy taxed to teach them better. I have not yet seen the newspaper which refers to those eminent bachelors, Noel Coward, Colonel T. E. Lawrence, Herr Hitler and the Prince of Wales as "this distressing type" —the words which Sir Oswald Mosley in the *Fascist Week* recently applied to unmarried women. In February 1934 Miss Helen Hope, writing in the *News-Chronicle*, set out to console a mother whose daughter of twenty-three was still unmarried, and kindly advised her not to dread too prematurely "the shadow of the manless thirties" darkening her darling's life. I have yet to read the journalistic consolation addressed to the bachelor in his twenties, though the shadow of "the womanless thirties" may possibly be cast by coming events over his projected programme.

The reason for this distinction is historical. The long concentration of women upon their domestic functions had for so many years deprived them when unmarried of normal activities and achievements that the popular mind came to associate a woman's marriage with her fulfilment. And conversely, without marriage she must remain "unfulfilled." Whereas neither sexual experience nor social activity for a man was presumed to depend upon his marriage. The double standard of morality expected all unmarried women to remain virgin, but cherished no such expectations for a bachelor. During times like the present when females are in considerable excess of males in Western Europe, popular legend evokes a picture of several million "superfluous" women—superfluous because each cannot have a husband, and in a monogamous society, is therefore mathematically destined to remain unmarried.

In actual fact, many circumstances may prevent this singleness from being at all unenviable. The spinster may have work which delights her, personal intimacies which comfort her, power which satisfies her. She may have known that rare light of ecstasy. In certain sections of society, it is possible that she will have had lovers. In Russia she may, without social disaster, have borne children. In most other countries unmarried mothers and their children are still placed under such social disadvantages that, however liberal their intellectual morality, their nerves are strained and their personality scarred as by calamity. Few individuals are strong enough to maintain poise and confidence and unselfconscious ease in the face of constant social criticism.

As for those unmarried women who remain virgins, some, highly-sexed by biological make-up, suffer physically. Their individual personality requires an activity which it has been denied. Others, never finding satisfactory occupation outside the domestic sphere, are constantly aware of the second-best position enjoyed by the unmarried woman in the home. But even more are affected, I think, by the pervasive and penetrating influence of opinion. The twentieth century having dethroned human reason set up the nerves and memory in their place. Freudian psychology has sanctioned the extreme veneration of sex. The followers of D. H. Lawrence have taught us to venerate instinct, emotion, and the intuitive vitality of the senses and to pity virgins for being unacquainted with a wide, deep and fundamentally important range of intuitive and sensual experience. They are taught to pity themselves. From their childhood they learn to dread the fate of "an old maid." In more sophisticated circles they anticipate a nemesis of "complexes." Puritan morality taught unmarried women that the loss of virginity doomed them to the torments of Hell in the next world; twentieth-century morality teaches them that the retention of virginity dooms them to the horror of insanity in this one. Thus, even when all their appetites for intimacy, power, passion and devotion are well satisfied, they must keep on asking themselves: "What am I missing? What experience is this without which I must—for I am told so—walk frustrated? Am I growing embittered, narrow, prudish? Are my nerves giving way, deprived of natural relaxation? Shall I suffer horribly in middle age? At the moment, life seems very pleasant; but I am an uncomplete frustrated virgin woman. Therefore some time, somewhere, pain and regret will overwhelm me. The psychologists, novelists, lecturers and journalists all tell me so. I live under the shadow of a curse."

A similar fear pursues the childless wife. Society, trained to safeguard its biological interests at a time when increase of population was desirable, will not let women choose. It dogs their steps, hounding them into marriage, into maternity, with the best intentions—and usually with the full co-operation of the women. But it will not let well alone. It continues to track down those who do not marry—(about 1 in 4 in modern England) and who do not have children, persuading them that their happiness is not happiness, their satisfaction not satisfaction, their preoccupations and interests a struggling and not too healthy sublimation.

So many women whose circumstances and temperament provide them with adequate material for happiness, are tormented by the current superstition that madness or bitterness lie in wait for virgins. The mystics were wiser when they recognised in celibacy not a deprivation but a power, for those who could win their satisfactions elsewhere. All flesh is not the same flesh. There is one glory of the sun and another glory of the moon and another glory of the stars; for one star differeth from another in glory.

If we did not suffer from a lamentable confusion of thought we should not allow one form of satisfaction to blind us to all others, and we should permit a more common and more merciful realisation of the fact that in the twentieth century frustration and spinsterhood need not be identical.

Do Modern Women make Good Mothers?

I forget which recent year was haunted by the rhythm of that idiotic yet somehow attractive song: "Do shrimps make good mothers?" with its emphatic rejoinder shouted in chorus: "Yes, they do!" Its nonsensical tune has rung in my head constantly as I survey the social phenomena of our time. It recurred to me when I read, in her challenging, fiercely honest book *No Time Like the Present*, one statement by Miss Storm Jameson with which I profoundly disagree. "In the end," she says, "the world is not yet a rap better because women have been let loose in it." We all know what she means by being let loose. Women have parliamentary votes, hold conferences, write newspaper articles, administer laws as county councillors, sit in judgment as magistrates, follow professions, direct industries, design advertisements.

The world at the moment is in a state of hysterical insanity. As I write Paris is rioting; there is civil war in

133   K

Austria; German prison camps are full of innocent but tormented men and women; Japan and Russia are discussing war; China is in confusion; there are bread queues in the United States; through the February fogs from Glasgow, Newcastle, Derby and Lancashire, the Hunger Marchers are limping, footsore if undaunted, towards London. Are these cruelties, threats, misfortunes, miseries the result of letting women loose in the world? Do they prove our impotence to restrain barbarism, preserve life, and maintain justice? Miss Jameson's accusation of failure is not unique. A popular journalist recently, commissioned to answer the question, "What has the vote done for me?" replied, "Nothing."

I think that they are wrong.

Quite apart from the increased self-confidence, freedom of judgment, interest and activity which women have won for themselves during the past fifty years—(a psychological revolution which, in spite of all set-backs and contradictions is still beyond adequate calculation)—the change of emphasis in social and political action since they acquired direct political influence has been enormous. It has been almost wholly on the side of increased amenities for public health, educational opportunity and domestic welfare. The people who maintain that woman's whole interest lies in domestic and humanitarian legislation are wrong. Under a system of identical education and complete freedom of action, their interests would probably be as multifarious as those of men—not only would an Amber Blanco-White turn naturally to banking, a Madame Kollantay to diplomacy, a Frances Perkins to Labour organisation but who knows how many to transport, agriculture and the conduct of public corporations. For centuries, however, the pendulum of governmental interest had swung away from the concerns of ordinary human life. Schools and hospitals, clinics and maternity benefit, medical inspection for juveniles, improved housing, the protection of children from assault and cruelty—the importance of these aspects of social organisation—had been almost completely neglected. It is since women have been "let loose in the world" that the neglect has been remedied to some still ludicrously small extent. It is still true that our political values are insanely lop-sided. But now that they are in public life, at least some women protest against the disproportion between our solicitude for the forces of destruction and our care for the constructive and civilized activities of the state.

Their protest has not been without effect. In November, 1933, the International Labour Organisation published an *International Survey of Social Services* based upon monographs prepared in twenty-four different countries. The material examined covered six subjects—population statistics, social insurance, social assistance, housing, family allowances and holidays with pay. The most interesting section, perhaps, dealt with social assistance, under which were grouped non-contributory pensions, unemployment relief, assistance for the blind and infirm, medical and maternity benefit, assistance for children, education and maintenance, and sickness benefits of various kinds. Some of the evidence is tragi-comic. Rumania, for instance, under Housing Statistics, observes that "In 1930, 74 dwellings were built as the result of an agreement with the Imprese Italiane all' Ester di Milano." 74 seems a trifle inadequate. But what is important is that almost all the immense structure of maternity, health, infant welfare, housing and sickness benefit has been constructed since the years when women became enfranchised. However shamefully inadequate these measures may be, it remains true that the German systems of youth officers, the Dutch system of welfare centres for the pre-school children, the British health services, the 1,274 Japanese child-welfare centres, the maternity benefits of Czecho-slovakia, have within 15 years to some small extent begun to redress a balance tilted the wrong way for two millennia.*

Do women make good parents? Not good enough, maybe, but so far as public organisation is concerned, better than men made while they had uncontested control of human affairs.

I have mentioned elsewhere Cicely Hamilton's remark that the twentieth century is the Age of the Child. It is also the first century in which women have had any voice in public organisation. I do not think the two facts disconnected.

At the same time, there is a tendency, popular in cheap journals and cheaper speeches, to suggest that modern mothers are neglectful. The Cinema, that illuminating guide to public sentiment, has an odd predilection for "silver-haired" mothers, while music-hall songs croon praises of "that old-fashioned mother of mine," as if new-fashioned mothers were less admirable.

As a matter of fact the "new-fashioned mother" takes her duties seriously. If she is really new-fashioned, her care for her children begins even before marriage. It is no longer considered indelicate for engaged girls before their wedding day to seek a medical examination, advice on sex hygiene, birth control, and consultation about hereditary or physiological peculiarities. Maternity to really modern mothers is not an accident; it is deliberately planned and provided for.

In this country after long delay and strenuous agitation by privately-supported organisations, local authorities are now permitted by the Ministry of Health to establish ante-natal clinics in which advice on contraception may be given to married women. Nor is it any longer a penal offence to receive such advice privately from general practitioners, while the sale and display of contraceptives is common enough. But it is still difficult to persuade the majority of

* See Appendix I, p. 195.

town and county councils to make use of their permissive authority. The old prejudice that contraceptive knowledge leads to sexual immorality, still reinforces opposition.

Nor is the use of contraceptives universal even among the women of countries where it is not illegal. One woman worker in a London maternity clinic told me that when offering advice about birth control to women already exhausted by too many children, again and again they repelled her with the words, "But it is so sordid!" The thought that it may be even more "sordid" to bring into an already over-crowded home, without proper means for their support, children predisposed to be sickly, under-nourished or unfit, has not yet overcome their traditional prejudice that forethought in sexual matters is indecent. But the practice of birth control is growing, in spite of passionate propaganda against it, by Catholics, big-population nationalists, prudes and upholders of the "non-inter-ference-with-nature" creed. In a speech in the House of Lords on February 13th, 1934, Lord Dawson of Penn declared that "the sale of contraceptives in this country had gone up by leaps and bounds. One firm at present turned out 8,500,000 a year, another turned out 72,000 a week, and that was reinforced by importation from abroad." Opponents of birth control talk as though these were used only to avoid the awkward consequences of fornication. Actually the great majority are bought by married couples anxious to bring children into the world only when they have planned their advent.

The control of parenthood does not stop at contra-ception. In the country where women are now most completely equal, and most intellectually free from a sense of inferiority, it is notable that they have also legalised abor-tion. In 1930 in Moscow alone 175,000 operations were performed, and the death rate amounted, according to a conservative estimate, to 1 in 20,000 cases. (Fannina Halle gives 1 in 25,000.) The immense number of cases points rather to absence of adequate knowledge of and means for contraceptive methods; it will certainly decrease as the latter become more easily obtainable. But, apart from the social significance of an innovation which at last removes that fundamental insecurity from a woman's life—the accidental incidence of pregnancy—the system has been adopted largely as a measure of child welfare. Soviet Russia has been sensible enough to recognise that unwanted children are a liability, not an asset, to the population.

But nowhere else is the mother's choice the decisive factor. Other countries have gone a certain way. Three years ago a bill on Russian lines was passed through the Lower House in Esthonia but was held up by the Executive. In Czecho-slovakia, where the Russian experiment was followed with keen interest, a similar bill was brought forward soon after the War by a Socialist woman deputy, Mme Landova Stychova; but failed to pass. A government measure, however, was later devised, which legalised abortion under certain conditions: if performed by a qualified physician in a public hospital, in cases where pregnancy and birth involved danger of death or permanent bodily injury to the mother, where rape has been legally proved, where a girl under sixteen has been criminally assaulted and made pregnant, where there is a probability of mental or physical defect in the child, where the woman is insane or mentally deficient and her guardians approve, and finally, where the pregnancy involves loss of food and care to the mother's other children.

As I write the passage of that law is uncertain, and its fate depends largely upon the extent to which Fascism with its "Big population" theory influences Czecho-slovakia; but in Poland, after vehement agitation, permission has been given to operate in cases of mental deficiency, pregnancy resulting from abuse of power by a relative or employer, rape, or grave danger to health. But such cases have all to go before special tribunals—a procedure which involves delay and often defeats its own ends.

In England the law is emphatic. Under Sections 58 and 59 of the Act of August 6, 1861, known as the "Offences against the Person Act," any pregnant woman who herself attempts to procure abortion by drugs or operative measures, is liable to "be kept in Penal Servitude for Life or for any term not less than three years, or to be imprisoned for any term not exceeding two years with or without hard labour and with or without solitary confinement," while any person wittingly helping her shall be liable to "be kept in Penal Servitude for the term of three years, or to be imprisoned for any term not exceeding two years, with or without hard labour."

Actually, the law is not kept. According to Mr. Justice McCardie "even surgical abortions are forbidden by the ludicrously wide terms of the Act." Such operations are now openly performed in cases where two or more doctors can be persuaded to sign a statement that a woman will die or become a hopeless invalid or lose her reason if she is permitted to bear her child at its natural period. But these cases are rare and some doctors refuse to go even thus far. What happens to-day is that the wealthy can find practitioners ready to take the risk of operating if the fee is high enough, and the poor attempt a dozen or more pernicious and often deadly substitutes for what has proved in Russia to be a simple and almost harmless surgical operation.

The Departmental Commission on Maternal Mortality in 1932 admitted that 47 per cent. of the 3,000 annual deaths in childbirth were preventable, and that beside these the amount of invalidism and injury both to parents and to children subsequently born, through unskilled and neglected abortion, is enormous. Here perhaps lies the real explanation of the failure to reduce the figures in maternal, as in infant, mortality.

Granted that human life is sacred, and that maternity is a racial task not to be shirked for fear of pain, desire for freedom, or dislike of sacrifice, the attempt here, as in many other cases, to "make people good by act of parliament" hardly seems to have succeeded. It is also questionable whether it is an act of virtue for a woman to bring into the world a child which is the fruit of rape or incest, which is predoomed to mental deficiency, or whose birth is bound to cost its mother's life or health. The fate of motherless children or of children in poor houses whose mothers are perpetual invalids, is not so enviable that one can blame their parents for seeking, even illegally, to avoid it.

In 1934, at the Hartlepool Conference of the Women's Co-operative Guild, the following resolution was sponsored by the Central Committee:

"In view of the persistently high maternal death rate and the evils arising from the illegal practice of abortion, this Congress calls upon the Government to revise the abortion laws of 1861 by bringing them into harmony with modern conditions and ideas, thereby making of abortion a legal operation that can be carried out under the same conditions as any other surgical operation. It further asks that women now suffering from imprisonment for breaking these antiquated laws be amnestied."

It was passed with only about 15 dissentient votes in an assembly of 1,360 working women.

The misery caused by the present state of affairs is so great, the effect on the health of the country so persistent and so undesirable, that sooner or later we shall have to change the law. One day we shall certainly think it barbarous that women in basement homes and squalid tenements, were permitted to torture themselves and jeopardise their lives with drugs and pills and all manner of inappropriate instruments, to prevent a sixth or seventh child coming to take the food from the mouths of the others, to prevent further malnutrition, mental deficiency or disease, to prevent, as they vainly hope, the permanent invalidism of the mother, because knowledge of contraception had been unavailable to her, and because the amenities of skilled attention were illegal.

In a perfect society no undesired child would be conceived. But this is an imperfect world, and when married couples sleep night after night together, constant abstention from intercourse exacts a nervous strain harmful to happiness and to the intimacy of human love; where methods of birth control are still imperfectly practised and, to many millions, unknown; where children, unwillingly conceived and resentfully carried, are born into poverty, disease and wretchedness, to become a burden on the community, and to swell the sad population in homes for mental defectives, sanatoria for the tuberculous, and poor law infirmaries. At present the very word "abortion" evokes a shock of nervous repugnance in most normal people. I cannot believe that this repugnance is divinely ordered or that its maintenance is ultimately essential for human welfare.

But many mothers at least attempt to bear their children when it shall be best for the child and best for themselves. They have also attempted to check the wastage of infant and maternity mortality. Not that this attempt has been wholly successful. Between 1920 and 1930 over 39,000 women died in childbirth in England and Wales alone. While the death rate from other causes (except war and road accidents) has steadily declined since 1900 in civilised countries, the rate for maternal mortality is almost stationary. But the infant death rate has fallen perceptibly; between 1905 and 1928 it dropped from 128 to 65 per 1,000 for children under one year in this country. The establishment of a Ministry of Health, of municipal Infant Welfare centres, of a 40s. maternity benefit under the National Insurance Acts, have done something towards making birth and infancy a less perilous adventure. The high rate of maternal mortality is partly due to economic conditions. Mothers who are under-nourished during pregnancy, who are encumbered with heavy housework and the care of older children, exhausted by anxiety and lack of sleep, who endure their labour in crowded, insanitary bedrooms, assisted by an over-pressed and often under-trained midwife, are not given a fair chance. But the slight difference between the maternal mortality rates in Mayfair and Bethnal Green suggests that obstetrical science is still immature, and that we need further knowledge of how to treat even those women who can secure all available resources of comfort and experience.

The whole national organisation of maternity services is still uneven and inadequate. In 1930 Miss Dorothy Jewson (ex-M.P.) reported that 186 Norfolk parishes had no arrangements for the supply of a midwife, while the rest relied largely on voluntary organisations. The Act of 1918 which establishes British Health services is only a permissive measure, allowing Local Authorities to establish Ante-natal Clinics, Health Visitors, Maternity Houses, Home Helps, the provision of extra food, nurses and convalescent homes, but not compelling them. Consequently everything depends on local initiative, which sometimes is non-existent.

But a beginning has been made. The amount of care and thought expended upon this business of bringing healthy and undamaged children into the world has never been surpassed. And England is by no means the most advanced country. Sweden, Italy, Holland, Norway, Uruguay, Denmark, Hungary and Japan have lower rates of maternal mortality. Holland possesses the finest maternity service in the world. The Midwifery Boards of Sweden enable their members to give far more individual attention to their patients than is usually possible here. Though public provision falls short, public imagination has been aroused, and the day of the drunken Sairy Gamp is passing.

It is true, too, that mothers are prepared to rely less on "mother instinct" and more upon scientific knowledge than they used to do. Not enough, of course. There is probably more nonsense talked about mother love and maternal intuition than about almost any other important subject. Proud grannies and mothers-in-law who have "buried seven" still lay down nursery lore in suburban villas and city mansions as well as in back-street tenements. But the conscientious solemnity with which most young mothers to-day study their responsibilities is admirable, even if sometimes a little misplaced. Experiments like the Chelsea Babies' Club are attempting to provide for middle-class families what the infant welfare clinics—where they exist —offer to the poor. Articles on diet, clothing, fresh air, temperament, minor ailments and other nursery problems, written with varying degrees of sense and authority, are an essential feature of most modern popular papers and magazines. Interest in child psychology is often carried to fantastic extremes; experimental schools, theories of discipline and no-discipline, of sex-education or no education, of environment and training, may become ridiculous rather than sublime; but they are at least less pernicious than the principles of the Fairchild Family, or the discipline of "good old-fashioned schools" where to spare the rod was to spoil the child, and where bullying, semi-starvation and constant physical discomfort were part of the traditional curriculum.

Maternity is considered so honourable that in its name divorce reform is delayed beyond all reason, women are underpaid, the education of many girls is crippled, women are denied the right of entry to posts which they could occupy with profit, or are forced to resign from work which they can do and which needs doing. On February 17th, 1934, Pastor Vera Kenmure, one of the earliest and most successful women Congregationalist ministers, wrote to resign her position.

"I do this most reluctantly," she said, "and only after much careful thought; but I feel that in the present circumstances it is the only course open to me.

"I wish to make it abundantly clear that I do not resign because I find the duties of a wife and mother are incompatible with those of the minister of a church. On the contrary I am convinced that my ministry, and indeed any ministry, will only be enriched and made more useful by the added experience which these relationships bring. Since my marriage I have carried out all my duties at Partick in the same spirit, and according to the same principles as before, and have continued such features of church life as midweek services at stated periods, a Bible Class conducted by myself, a Young Communicants' Class, and one evening per week in the Vestry when I am available for consultation, some of which were introduced in the church for the first time during my term of office. All these, of course, were in addition to the general offices of the church.

"My sole reason for resigning is my strong feeling that the deep opposition and active hostility of a section of the congregation make honest co-operation impossible, and prevent me from continuing a successful ministry among them. I will not be the minister of any church where disharmony is rife."

The Congregational Church nearly lost a good minister; a devoted religious personality nearly lost a clear vocation. Actually, after a brief interval, the congregation organised an appeal for their minister to return. When I write, the controversy has not yet been settled. But so long as a mingled odour of sentimentality and obscenity is allowed to envelop the idea of motherhood, we shall have to endure episodes of this kind.

The attitude towards older children, too, is changing.

The relationship between parent and child is more natural, more candid, and more democratic. The parents take a positive rather than negative interest in their children's health and temperament. It is not enough for Fenella or Robert to "get through" measles or mumps or other childish ailments with the least possible trouble to everyone. It is not enough for them to avoid conspicuous "naughtiness." To-day there are attempts to investigate and remove possible causes of physical or mental handicap—from flat feet and constipation to fear of the dark and the Œdipus complex. There is, I think, less possessiveness and more comradeship, less discipline and more understanding, less fuss and more instructed care. When families are smaller, when women have educated minds and wider interests, when husband and wife alike control the family income, this individual attention is more possible. The professional woman, or intelligent artisan's wife to-day, puts far more common sense and organising ability into her maternal responsibility than the Victorian lady, worn out by successive miscarriages and births, doomed to premature invalidism on a sofa, who was so frequent a "Mamma" in the books I read in my nursery days. Mothers who can share their children's interests, mothers who have some knowledge of the wider world outside the family circle, are far better equipped than purely domestic housewives, to help their sons and daughters as they pass from school to the shops and offices and factories and universities in which they complete their education.

Incidentally, these mothers are far more popular with their children. I dare to speak from experience. My own mother, though born over seventy years ago, is essentially "modern." As a county alderman, she finds life rich with varied and absorbing experience. I can visit or leave her without compunction, knowing that she has her life to live as much as I have mine; yet when we meet there is none of that awkwardness, that "making conversation" which I see between so many parents and children. In the future the child will be as much interested in the mother's career as the mother in the child's, and the shared experience of two generations should be helpful to both.

Do women of the twentieth century—like shrimps— make good mothers? So far as generalisation is possible I I think that we can answer in the words of the song: "Yes, they do!"

The Cost of Housekeeping.

In Soviet Russia where shortage of houses at present makes home life in the cities impossible for hundreds of families, the equality of women's status is more unequivocally and openly acknowledged than in any other contemporary state.

The facts are not necessarily interdependent. There is for instance little home life, as interpreted by the Ideal Homes Exhibition or by popular American advertisements, in the tents of nomadic Mahometans of Southern Arabia; yet women there live in semi-slavery. But neither are the circumstances completely unconnected.

For the tradition of woman as home-maker encumbers her intellectual and economic progress at every turn. It even incommodes her attempts to become an adequate wife to her husband and mother to her children. For the sake of human happiness, justice, intelligence and welfare, I should like to see all family homes and amateur housekeepers abolished for the space of one generation; because at present the price we pay for these luxuries is too high. We pay for them in humbug and irritation; we pay in narrowing down our interests and our loyalties; we pay in the deliberate stultifying of our human growth. Most of all, we pay in an orgy of vicious and enervating self-deception. We shall never really be able to live comfortably in homes till we have destroyed the legend of their sanctity.

Naturally there is value in the domestic arts. Food

should be well prepared, rooms should be clean and charming, clothes decently repaired, a civilised standard of comfort and of order preserved in every dwelling place. Nor need the performance of these functions be disagreeable. On the contrary, they provide scope for faculties of ingenuity and of taste ; they are varied; they produce immediate and obvious results, and they are valuable. Those who perform them know that they are contributing to social happiness. We need places where children may feel secure and adults rested, at ease from the critical, competitive public life where they are constantly forced to measure up to one another, to put something across, to push something through, or exert their personalities to avert some failure.

Because these things are desirable, however, that does not mean that they are worth any price we choose to pay for them. What, exactly, is this price?

In the first place our illusion that every woman generally and every married woman particularly must become a housekeeper causes a preposterous waste of time, and distortion of activity. The traditional inquiry of the love-lorn swain, "Can she cook a cherry-pie, charming Billy?" interprets itself into the surviving supposition that, whatever other functions a woman may fulfil, whether she be doctor, cotton-spinner, member of parliament or shopkeeper, she will naturally hold herself responsible for the catering, cleaning, laundry work and care of children in the household where she lives. Even to-day when she may be providing the major part of the family income, it is still her business to see that meals are prepared, invalids nursed, hospitality arranged, nurseries organised and comfort secured. Husbands and brothers and fathers feel themselves aggrieved, if, with "a woman about the house" any domestic burden still falls on their shoulders, and proposals for communal performance of work now done individually are received with shocked disapproval.

Even efficiency of organisation, by which a professional woman could delegate much of the routine of housekeeping, is so commonly regarded as a defection that she sacrifices real comfort to a social ideal which profits nobody. She would rather dust rooms than feel guilty. The tradition is a natural legacy from the days when women provided the work and men the money in all average homes; but when traditions persist after facts have changed, injustice inevitably occurs.

But if it is true that many women better equipped to be engineers, lawyers or agricultural workers, waste their time on domestic activities, which husbands, sons or professional employees might more effectively perform, it is even more true that other women who are naturally inclined to enjoy domestic work, use it as an excuse to do nothing and know nothing else. The consciousness of virtue derived from well-polished furniture or rows of preserved-fruit bottles is too lightly acquired. In too many small homes women use the domestic tradition to evade responsibility for everything else. "Oh, I'm only a housekeeper. I'm a private person. My job lies within four walls," they say complacently, finding it easier to be a good housewife than a good citizen. So long as their own children are healthy and happy, why worry because others are ill and frightened? It is agreeable to distemper one's own nursery, bake crusts, squeeze oranges and mix nourishing salads; it is not agreeable to sit on quarrelling committees, listen to tedious speeches, organise demonstrations and alter systems, in order that others—for whom such wholesome pleasures are at present impossible—may enjoy them. Yet women are praised for the maternal instinct which makes the care expended on their own children natural and pleasant; they are criticised for the political activities which result in the safeguarding of other people's children as well as their own. So slums remain uncleared, milk is wasted, nursery schools are exceptional luxuries, educational reforms are delayed, while "good wives and mothers" shut themselves up in the comfort of their private lives and earn the approval of unthinking society.

Such limitation defeats its own ends. It is like the barrier which another type of woman erects between herself and the reality of love and intimacy. In the luxury flats of 1934 as in the palaces of 1734, live women whose lives are dominated by so specialised an ideal of personal beauty that the very manifestations of life which beauty is meant to vitalise, become distasteful to them.

But if some women enclose themselves from the world in their homes as in a nunnery, there are others who, finding their energies disproportionate to the limited sphere of domestic action, make their houses little Hells of restlessness. They do twice what needs to be done once; they fuss over details of punctuality, laundry and ornament; they bully their families or servants into neuroses; they disfigure every piece of furniture with embroidery or decoration, and invent a hundred hideous and superfluous activities to occupy their unfilled hours.

One result of this energy affects the home itself. It becomes far too elaborate and remains far too inconvenient. Women's unacknowledged fear lest, robbed of domestic work, they should find no real function in life, does unceasing damage to standards of domestic architecture and furnishing. It has retarded the whole progress of scientific labour-saving. The most inferior factory architect would be ashamed to submit plans accepted as adequate for domestic purposes—the sink in a dark corner, the oven and stove where backs are ricked to reach them, the plumbing primitive and furniture designed to attract a maximum of dust.

Yet every year standards grow higher. Just as we have repudiated in horror the legendary method of measuring the baby's bath water—("I pops the blessed bairn in and if it's too cold he turns blue and if it's too hot he turns red.")

—so we have abandoned many other rough-and-ready devices. Conscientious and well-to-do housewives like conscientious and well-to-do mothers, burden themselves with entire libraries on colour schemes, cocktail recipes, and etiquette for the week-end party; while working-class women, with more elaborate furniture bought on the hire-purchase system, advice from health visitors and infant welfare instructors, and articles in the popular press, give themselves three times the work done by their more primitive predecessors. Women really determined to spend no more time than was absolutely necessary upon domestic labour could have revolutionised housekeeping within a decade.

There is a reverse side to the same picture. Paradoxically the very people who neglect to apply science to the home, think far too much of comfort, or respectability and of "keeping up appearances." They measure social worth by the lampshades in the drawing-room, the parlour-maid who answers the door, and the wine served at dinner-parties. This is not by any means an exclusively female folly. Men as much as women devote themselves to the ritual rather than the spirit of hospitality, sacrifice vitality for comfort, and comfort to conformity. They turn their houses into temples where the gods of respectability and decorum can be worshipped. And we all suffer.

Wives suffer from their servitude to an ideal unworthy of exclusive service. Why, in entertainments of the well-to-do, does general conversation so often hang, spiked upon the uncomprehending inattention of the "wives" who sit among the men and women? Why should there be so little give and take of argument and opinion in most families? Why should mothers lose touch with the interests of their growing sons and daughters?

Unmarried women suffer—from their identification with domesticity.

Men suffer—from boredom, loneliness, and surfeit of comfort. We pay too high a price for our good housekeeping.

CHAPTER IV

BACKWARDS AND FORWARDS

DURING the spring of 1934 a well-known political organisation in London asked a friend of mine to lecture on the subject of "The Rise of Anti-Feminism in Europe." She gave the lecture but changed the title. There was no "rise of anti-feminism" in Europe, she declared. There had been a rise of feminism; there is now a reaction against it. The pendulum is swinging backwards, not only against feminism, but against democracy, liberty, and reason, against international co-operation and political tolerance.

Yet on the whole the situation for women is more hopeful and certainly more comfortable than it was a hundred years ago. Even the new antagonisms have their advantages.

Definite opposition is easier to break than unacknowledged obstruction. Sir Walter Scott retold in *The Talisman* the old story of how Richard I and Saladin set out to compete in skill of swordsmanship. King Richard lifted his sword and brought it down with a great crash, splitting in two a suit of armour; but Saladin tossed a silken cushion into the air, and while it floated feather-light, cut it in half with a dexterous twist of his curved blade—a far more difficult feat. For thirteen years women have been smothered by silken cushions of persuasion; they may find the hard iron of compulsion easier to resist.

Herr Hitler finds a cure for Unemployment

The example of reaction most constantly quoted is that of Nazi Germany. It is the most conspicuous, the most deliberate and the most characteristic. When in the autumn of 1933 the British Industrialist, Sir Herbert Austin, acknowledged his desire to turn all women out of his employment and replace them by men, he quoted the example of Herr Hitler. Just because in Germany the Woman's movement appeared to have progressed so far, the retrogression appeared peculiarly significant.

The Constitution of the German Republic drawn up at Weimar in 1918, wrote equality of rights into its fundamental laws.

Article 109 ran:

"All Germans are equal before the law. Men and women have, in principle, the same civil rights and duties."

And Article 128:

"All citizens, without discrimination, shall be eligible for public office.

"All provisions making exception in the case of women officials shall be abolished."

Women immediately began to take advantage of their new opportunities. From 30 to 42 sat in each of the Reichstags between 1919 and 1933—a higher proportion than in any other country. Women became provincial councillors and ministers. They entered into every kind of occupation, winning distinction as administrators, teachers, scientists and technicians. In the 1925 census, 11,478,000 German women were registered as employed, of whom 3,645,000 were married. They organised trade unions. They took part in international conferences. They explored, with unusual earnestness and deliberation, the social implications of economic independence. They entered with immense enthusiasm into the new athletic movements. The typical "modern girl" of post-War Germany was a lean young creature, browned with sun-bathing, muscular, vigorous, who earned her own living, held theories about free love which shocked her parents, who spent her holidays tramping across country in shorts and shirt, and believed that Communism might inaugurate an earthly paradise.

But the background of her life was far from happy. The German heart was sick with hope deferred; eleven million women might be employed. In Germany as in England of the Slump, and for the same reasons, it was easier for women than for men to obtain work. The humiliations of Versailles persisted. The country remained unarmed in an armed continent. Even after 1926, when her representatives were greeted at Geneva and the state received into the League of Nations, when M. Briand exclaimed in one of his most moving orations: "C'est fini, la guerre entre nous," the brave words remained words alone; their promises were not fulfilled. It became impossible to cope adequately with the feeding and housing of the workless. The unemployment figures rose in February, 1932 to 6,128,429.

In 1933 Herr Hitler came into power largely on his promise to revive German vitality and national prosperity, and to solve the unemployment problem. Now the simplest solution of that problem is to proclaim large sections of the community unemployable and to withdraw them from the labour market altogether.

Thus in England proposals have been made to relieve the pressure by raising the school-leaving age to 16, and by reducing to 60 the age at which insured persons may receive old-age pensions—thus draining from employment the very young and very old. In America the Roosevelt administration has attempted to reduce the quite considerable extent of child-labour with the same intention.

But the German experiment goes further than that. National Socialist philosophy, with its doctrines of racial solidarity, biological mysticism and the Functional State, makes possible a far more sweeping clearance from the labour market. Non-Aryans, Jews and Pacifist-Com-

munist-Left-Wing-Socialist-Intransigeants have been compulsorily removed to make room for loyal Nazi Germans.
But compulsion creates its own difficulties. A far more
ingenious solution has been found in the persuasion of
women to leave the labour market willingly, under a
psychological pressure applied with formidable effect.

The explanation of the women's readiness to go is largely
historical. The post-War economic independence of
women was not only more novel in Germany than it was
in England; it was more disturbing. Far more deeply-
rooted in German than in English consciousness was the
tradition that women's interests should be confined to
"Kinder, Küche, Kirche." The political theories of democracy, liberty and toleration, which lent so strong a support
to the women's movement in this country had less influence there. All the time that the younger German women
were reaching out towards a new philosophy of personal
and political and economic relationships, their elders were
opposing to it a fervour of conviction and a solidarity of
family influence rarely experienced in England or America.

The proof of the pudding lies in the eating. The taste of
independence had not been so sweet. Husbands, sons and
fathers remained without employment. Lovers dared not
marry. Men grew increasingly and justifiably embittered.
There seemed no adequate answer to their criticisms of a
national condition which left them without hope. Prosperity dwindled and courage waned.

When, therefore, Herr Hitler preached a Functional
State with a place for everyone, a new World Philosophy
of disciplined unity, and a foreign policy which would
restore German honour and prestige, it was not surprising
that the women as well as the men accepted him. Even
though it meant economic dependence and psychological
docility, for women his doctrines promised a happiness
impossible under the earlier regime.

The method of political subjection has been, on the

whole, quite skilful and effective. German women have not been disenfranchised, though there was some talk in 1933 of their being "invited" to surrender their parliamentary vote. But all enfranchisement has been rendered meaningless under a system which permits only one political party. The provincial assemblies have not functioned, and no woman's name was on the candidates' list of National Socialists to be returned to the Reichstag. No woman occupies a position of importance in the government, though one, Paula Seiber, is associated with the Ministry of the Interior as adviser upon women's questions, and another, Hedwig Fuerster, reports upon matters concerning girls' schools to the Prussian Minister of Arts, Sciences and Public Instruction.

But the economic replacement has been more brutal and direct. Women are being increasingly excluded from educational administration. Since July 1933 the management of all girls' high schools in Hamburg has been transferred to men. Nineteen women directors of elementary schools have been replaced. The paper *Germania* in its issue of August 3, 1933, reported that 160 women teachers were then dismissed in Hamburg.

Married women doctors are no longer allowed to attend insured patients—a fairly effective means of driving them out of practice. "Double earnings" have been rigorously condemned, and daughters of men on pension as well as wives of wage-earners have been forced to resign under this excuse. Local authorities and private firms have dismissed women from law courts, offices, shops and factories, giving their posts to masculine members of the party.

To soften these harsh measures, every step has been taken to encourage women's domestic interests. Families employing domestic servants no longer have to contribute towards their sickness insurance. A government loan of 1,000 marks is offered to every woman who, having been a wage-earner for six months or more, marries, retires, and undertakes to accept no new position unless her husband's salary falls below 125 marks a month. In one Hamburg cigarette factory six hundred women were asked to give up their posts to fathers, brothers and husbands. Sixty did as requested and eighty, handing over their work to fiancés, claimed the state marriage loan; the others refused to leave.

A steady pressure of influence has accompanied these actions. Scientists have undertaken to prove that professional women produce a lower birth rate than those without such double activities. (A controversy over this point arose in *Die Aerztin* during August 1933, and though the theory was discredited by unquestionable evidence, it left its mark.) Attempts have been made to centralise all women's organisations under the "Women Workers' League," led by men, with Dr. Frick, the Minister for Home Affairs as Patron. Its president is Dr. Fermmacher, who recently stated that "The withdrawal of women from political activities and reawakening of a good German family life is of the first importance." Dr. Goebbels has announced that women have absolutely nothing to do with politics—though he received some applause for a statement that German ladies should not be reproved for smoking—a concession to gallantry as ominous as his more candid generalisation.

But far more important than official policy, which is at least open to public criticism, is the attitude of the women themselves. There are rebels. Some have been forced to leave the country. Others have been dismissed from their posts and live on private charity. Others attempt with immense courage, considering the rigour of discipline, to make public protest. For instance in *Volkischer Beobachter* of October 4th, 1933, one woman writer exposed the fallacy of the attempt to deal with unemployment by turning women out of their posts. "A woman without private

means and without work is also one of the unemployed
and a charge to the public," she wrote. "She herself bears
the burden of a heavy destiny. To turn away a woman
who has to find work, and to replace her by a man is not
the creation of new employment." It is, one would
imagine, a self-evident statement; but passion and prejudice can over-ride arithmetic. A few keen supporters of
the new regime dare to oppose its anti-feminism. One,
Carola Struve, wrote a book defending Hitler, but claiming, among other things, that the complete economic freedom for women was "the basis of their communal life
with men." Another sent a protest to Hitler and von
Papen against "the conversion of the new Germany into
a man-governed state."

But for the most part, the German women submit.
They have always followed fashions and this is a fashion.
They have always accepted discipline, and this is the order
of authority. They have always been seduced by theory,
and this has able apologists to rationalise it.

In November 1933, a letter appeared in the *Manchester
Guardian* from a German apologist of her government's
policy. "The German people," she wrote, "led by their
great Fuhrer, are to-day labouring for the re-birth of the
nation and of morals. They know perfectly well that this
task invests women with at least the same importance as
men. The young generation obtain their first nourishment
and teaching from their mothers. For this reason woman
has again been recognised as the centre of family life and
to-day it has again become a pleasure and an honour to be
a woman. We women of Germany have therefore
regained our confidence and faith in the future." Ques-
tioned further in private correspondence she gave no explanation of why it had ever ceased to be "a pleasure and
an honour to be a mother"; but she did maintain that there
was no hardship in the dismissal of women, who were still
allowed to follow "just such professions and vocations as

are suitable for their female gifts, i.e. which correspond to their maternal character. . . . Recognising our peculiarities we have chosen certain callings as specially suited. But I must stress that legally no vocation or profession is closed to us. . . . Do you really believe that a *weltanschauung* which inscribes on its banners that mothers are to be honoured does not result in women being treated with the greatest respect? . . . Herr Hitler is the exponent of a *weltanschauung*. The question of women or rather the question of the stability of family life forms part of this philosophy. . . ."

The reaction is explicable.

The slump, the Peace Treaties, the inefficiency of democratic administrations in a country with autocratic traditions, the deeply-ingrained social theories of feminine subservience, and the inconveniencies of a disunited nation provide motive enough for acceptance of Herr Hitler's policy. The Fuhrer himself, with Count Keyserling, Spengler, Sieburg and other prophets of the decline of the West, invent noble justification. In any case, German women are handing back political power and economic opportunity to the men.

The Intellectuals despair of Reason

Events in contemporary Germany would be less important did they not march with fashionable and world-wide theory. The passionate protests of Sieburg, the grave sententious mysticism of Count Keyserling, the inarticulate apologists for National Socialism strike a note which had already become familiar to Europe and America.

The insistence upon racial solidarity, instinctive unity, "blood-thought" and intuitive functionalism preached to-day from Munich to Posen is only one expression of a revolt against reason which has affected the intellectual life of the entire Western World. It has been traced to a dozen different sources—to a resurgence of the subconscious intuitive self from long suppression, to the publication of

Pascal's *Pensées* or of Bergson's *Creative Evolution*, to the psychology of Freud and the art of D. H. Lawrence, to the Expressionists, to the Nudists, to the scientists, to the war. But whatever its cause, there is little doubt that a mistrust of the intellect has been let loose in the world, and especially among the intellectuals.

It touches unexpected spheres of influence, from the evangelical revivalism known as the Group Movement, to the restless intellectualism of Aldous Huxley. "The heart has its reasons which the intellect knows not of," declared Pascal, and Huxley, Santanyana, General Goering and Mr. Buchman, in their varying modes, agree.

It finds political expression in revived enthusiasm for Nationalism, in contempt for democracy, in an outcry for a leader. Throughout the work of D. H. Lawrence, the self-appointed poet and prophet of the movement, that demand for leadership recurs. " 'Men,' says Lilly to Aaron in *Aaron's Rod*, 'must submit to the greater soul in a man for their guidance: and women must submit to the positive power-soul in man for their being.'

" 'You'll never get it,' said Aaron.

" 'You will, when all men want it. All men say, they want a leader. Then let them in their souls *submit* to some greater soul than theirs. At present, when they say they want a leader, they mean they want an instrument, like Lloyd George. A mere instrument for their use. But it's more than that. It's the reverse. It's the deep fathomless submission to the heroic soul in a greater man.' "

Compare that demand to General Goering's affirmation in his book *Germany Reborn*.

"In Hitler we have the rare combination of a keen logical thinker, a really profound philosopher and an iron-willed man of action, tenacious to the highest degree. . . . For more than a decade I have stood at his side, and every day spent with him is a new and wonderful experience. From the first moment that I saw and

heard him I belonged to him body and soul, and to many
of my comrades the same thing has happened. I pas-
sionately pledged myself to his service and have followed
him unswervingly. In the past months I have received
many titles and honours, but no title or honour has so
filled me with pride as the title which the German people
have given me: 'The most loyal lieutenant of our
Leader.'"

All over the world to-day, men and women, fatigued by
the austere struggle to serve ideas, are seeking for a man to
whom they can surrender their wills—for "the submission
to the heroic soul in a greater man." And in Germany,
Italy, Turkey, Poland perhaps, Russia while Lenin lived,
they have found one. The worship of Lenin had just this
difference. He himself was high priest of a religion of
rationalism; Marxian communism survived his death.

But a world of hero-worshippers is a world in which
women are doomed to subordination. Very rare exceptions, a Queen Elizabeth or Joan of Arc may capture men's
imagination. For the most part society takes care to see
that the Leader is masculine. The peculiar nature of this
cult demands it. Virility, combativeness, physical endurance, power to impress all types of person, are the qualities
demanded, and since quite sixty per cent. of humanity is
at present irremediably predisposed against submission to a
woman, the odds are enormous.

Socially the cult expresses itself in the lauding of the
instincts and the emphasis of "biological," "natural," or
"traditional" values. Since reason and the intellect have
fallen into disfavour, the instincts are accounted as of
higher importance than the mind. Passion, which Hegel
called "a sort of instinct, almost animal, by which man
applies his energies to a single cause," becomes associated
almost exclusively with physical desire, and the difference
between the sexes is necessarily exaggerated.

Since what has happened in Germany is not unique, it

may be worth while to consider the attitude of our most conspicuous English candidate for the dictatorship. Sir Oswald Mosley in 1932 devoted a short section of his statement on policy, *The Greater Britain*, to "Women's Work."

"It has been suggested," he began modestly, "that in our political organisation we have hitherto concentrated on the organisation of men. This was not because we underrate the importance of women in the world. . . . The part of woman in our future organisation will be important, but different from that of men; *we want men who are men and women who are women.*" The italics are Sir Oswald's; they are, I think, important. They illustrate that emphasis upon sexual difference characteristic of a creed which places instinct above reason. "Fascism," he continues, "would treat the normal wife and mother as one of the main pillars of the State," and he is gently sportive about "professional spinster politicians"; whose one idea is to escape from "the normal sphere of woman." Professional bachelor politicians like Herr Hitler presumably do not escape from the normal sphere of man. It is man's "natural" sphere to dominate. From that state of exaltation which Mr. Wyndham Lewis writing before Hitler's ascendancy described among his followers as "a true bodily solidarity, identical rhythms in the arteries and muscles and in the effective neural instrument," women are excluded. The bloodbrotherhood leaves them outside, quiescent, passive, waiting obediently to refresh the tired warrior.

They have been cast, in the functional state, for the rôle of wives, mothers, expectant and desirous mistresses. The whole force of the Freudian revelation, the "modern" morality and the fashionable insistence upon nerves rather than reasons, lies behind that choice. They have been told that without complete physical satisfaction they will remain dwarfed and crippled. They have been taught that the ubiquitous Eye in the once familiar Scriptural text "Thou God seest me" is blind and merciful in comparison to the jealous watchfulness of the frustrated sub-conscious. Jehovah the all Terrible might forgive; the instincts have no mercy. There is no appeal from their inexorable judgment.

Therefore let them take their appointed place in society and be satisfied.

It is true that they will be cut off from a hundred fields of action. It is true that they will be separated from their friends and lovers by a gulf of sexual difference. If no bridge of reason is considered trustworthy, if no shared experience of all those vast areas of life unaffected by sexual distinction may unite them, then indeed the ways of men and women become strange to one another. Woman remains a "mystery"; man an inscrutable "power," and though mystery may have its fascination, the comradeship of sympathy and understanding is destroyed.

But this is part of the new gospel, and women must take comfort from the traditionalists who tell them that—save for mad moments of irresponsible experiment—this has always been so.

For to reinforce their arguments, the anti-rationalists envoke tradition. In his brilliant and persuasive attack upon reason called *Toryism and the Twentieth Century* Mr. Walter Elliot, M.P., described the attitude of himself and those who felt with him as a "Belief in a humility of the intellect, and therefore a trust in continuity, a conviction that what has worked once may work again, and finally a certain optimism, believing that external forces are on the whole friendly to man, that they are good, albeit good and irrational; in fact that, though they slay us, yet will we trust in them."

But tradition is against equality. If in the future we are to rely only upon what has happened in the past, experiment is closed to us. The adventures of the mind must be abandoned. The attempt to create communities where men and women alike share the full stature of humanity is an attempt to do something which has not been done before, and which can only be achieved under certain conditions. And one of these is the acceptance of reason as a guide in human conduct. If we choose an anti-rational philosophy, in this quest, at least, we are defeated. The enemies of reason are inevitably the opponents of "equal rights."

Nationalism and the Jingo

Closely allied to the unpopularity of reason lies the popularity of nationalism. The nation is defended as a traditional, instinctive unit, something to which men feel themselves bound by blood and history. It has, like all great sacramental symbols, been sanctified by death. Its appeal is to the emotion rather than the intellect.

Nationalism in itself might be a neutral influence upon the position of women. Indeed, in some countries it has acted as an additional impetus to their emancipation. In India to-day the National Congress movement is one of the strongest forces for breaking a slave tradition. Women whose parents accepted unquestioningly the principles of sati and purdah, have left their seclusion, unveiled their faces, picketed shops, attended public meetings, and walked in processions. Customs of submission and confinement, centuries old, have been abandoned.

Nor is Indian experience unique. In Egypt, in Turkey, in Arabia, nationalism has aroused women from their long relegation to the status of semi-slavery. The need for citizenship has proved stronger than the barrier of sex.

This is true. It is true also that Jingoism and military values, which, under a system of international anarchy are inevitably associated with nationalism, have not always exercised an inimical effect upon women's position. We have to reckon with the immense sweep of world opinion which changed constitutions and customs alike between 1914 and 1918. We have to admit also that in modern

Russia, where the state is organised as a fighting unit, and where women are admitted into the Red Armies, the boldest experiments of equalitarian status have been carried through.

So far as modern war is concerned, the old division of interest between men and women has disappeared. Civilian populations of to-day suffer with armies in territories in which war is fought; to-morrow, they may suffer even more. The distinction between combatant and non-combatant decreases, and the qualifications of the combatant lose their dominatingly masculine traits. When the need for muscular strength diminishes women can be soldiers as well as men. In the last war British and American women drove cars, and performed clerical and domestic and technical work at the base, as well as serving medical and nursing units; while in Russia and the Balkan states, as in China, some fought as actual combatants. Even to-day in England Commandant Allen's Women's Auxiliary Detachment offers women training in aircraft and marksmanship. In future struggles where, we are told, laboratory work and aviation will play as large a part as gunnery and trench warfare, there is likely to be less and less distinction between men's part and women's part.

War ceases to become a masculine occupation.

Nor is it true that the non-military aspects of life commonly described as "women's interests" are exclusively feminine. Men also have been helpless as children, require shelter, nourishment, education and medical attention. And it is these requisites of humanity which suffer eclipse under a military system.

The cost of the annual defence bill of Great Britain is about £108,000,000—one quarter of which spent on smoke abatement, water supply, better housing and milk distribution could raise appreciably the whole standard of life in this country. Twenty thousand new houses could be built for the cost of one modern battleship. During the last war, the preliminary bombardments of Arras, Messines and Paschendale cost £52,000,000. Mr. Arthur Greenwood, Minister of Health in the Labour Government, worked out the cost of his proposed national maternity service at £2,750,000 a year. For the price of three bombardments we could have had a maternity service for nearly 20 years.

But these values predominate political thought almost everywhere to-day. Protests against them have hitherto had little practical effect. Until a system of world order and collective security is established, they will continue to dominate us.

And while they dominate, it is not easy for women to exercise completely equal citizenship, because, though it is true that militarism is not necessarily masculine and humanitarianism is not by any means intrinsically feminine, yet for so many years war has been considered a man's business, and the safeguarding of the interests of the helpless—of children, invalids and the very poor, a woman's, that the association of ideas still exerts a powerful influence over imaginations. Rightly or wrongly, this is what popular sentiment approves, and behind popular sentiment is something stronger. Maternal instinct as a political impulse has been greatly over-rated. The uneducated instinct generally seems to operate by urging women to protect their own children at whatever cost to others; but that it can be developed into a powerful sense of public responsibility has been shown by the brief history of women's influence in politics. The combination of motives which makes women politically "good mothers" makes them also comparatively poor soldiers. Under wholly different circumstances and after several generations these distinctions might disappear. But to-day they make it fairly clear that a woman is less likely to become a great admiral than a great Minister of Education or Organiser of Health Services. She is far less likely to acquire the experience and authority for naval leadership, even if she formed the taste for it. There are women with a taste for military discipline. The caréers of Commandant Mary Allen in this country or of Comrade Petrova the sixty-year-old storm trooper of Kerensky's Army in Siberia, mother of nine children and veteran of two wars, may be exceptional; but we have little evidence to prove that they would remain so were the ranks of armies, navies and air forces universally thrown open to women, and as little prejudice opposing their recruitment as to-day opposes that of men. Whether this would be a good thing or not for civilization is another question, though personally I see no reason why, if wars are to be fought at all, women should not be subject to conscription, service and death on the same terms as men. They suffer misery enough from war as it is, and suffer also from the inferiority of status which a non-combatant earns. If they are to endure the suffering, they might as well be spared the humiliation.

Mussolini and the Population Theory

One of the theories, however, associated with militant nationalism, has a very direct and vital effect upon the position of women, and that is what Miss Cicely Hamilton in her book on *Modern Italy* called "The Cult of the Cradle." In Italy, in Germany, in Ireland and in France to-day fecundity is revered as a patriotic virtue. Babies are potential citizens and potential soldiers. Ultimately the state with the largest population comes out on top. The mother who fills the cradle enables her sovereign to rule the world.

Signor Mussolini has his own clear notions of women's place in the world. His biographer Margherita Sarfatti records admiringly that the Duce regards woman as "a creature whose mission it is to be beautiful and pleasing. . . . If she does not know that she pleases she is nervous and unhappy, and with good reason." Therefore he encourages women to become Fascisti. They may join the Fasci

Femminili. But their groups are separate from and subordinate to the men's groups. Their activities include the relief of distress, child welfare and Red Cross work, and their drills and exercises are, from childbirth, given a domestic and maternal bias.

These public activities are, however, merely pleasant accessories to their great aim in life—the production of more and yet more Italian patriots. There is a tax on bachelors, to encourage early marriage. Taxation is graded to discriminate against one-child or childless marriages and in favour of the teeming nursery. Bonuses for large families, for twins, for triplets are the gifts of the state to dutiful mothers. With greater imagination than that exhibited by public authorities in this country. Italian officials do not compel women to resign from paid employment upon marriage. On the contrary, since June 1929 in state and provincial posts, preference has been given to married employees of both sexes. It is recognised that mothers may find it advisable, for their children's sake, to earn money to provide better food, clothes and lodging. There are times when even the day-long attention of a devoted parent fails to compensate for lack of vitamins—a fact still hidden from the wisdom of the London County Council when it compels married women employees to resign their posts. Further, large families are encouraged by revenue concessions, by free municipal services, and most of all by an atmosphere of public approval.

No state perhaps has yet developed so deliberate and systematised a population cult as Fascist Italy, though Nazi Germany seeks the multiplication of loyal Teutonic Aryans, France, the reproduction of healthy citizens, Southern Ireland, poor as it is, the increase of Catholic Celts, and in all Anglo-Saxon countries live individuals dominated by Lothrop Stoddard's fear of the "Rising Tide of Colour," who look to a recrudescence of White Births to counter the alarming fecundity of the black and yellow races. The cult of the cradle, in one form or another, affects women almost everywhere, even where it fails to receive government support.

Respect for maternity is naturally not in itself a bad thing for women. The German defender of Hitler's *Weltanschauung*, whose letter I previously quoted, clearly felt that here was the first necessity for human happiness. It is probable that the ancient fertility cults and recurrent mother-worship served to quench the pagan fears of women's "uncleanness" and of those mysterious magic influences which could blight virility and drain masculine strength. An enlightened sense of responsibility towards the unborn generations of the future may be one of the by-products of this desire for vicarious extension of life— this hope of family, tribal or national heirs.

It is equally true that English society to-day suffers from lack of respect for maternity. Every brand of saccarine sentiment is poured over motherhood and infancy. But the little done to encourage willing and successful maternity is one of the wonders of our astonishing age. We tolerate houses which offer no accommodation for perambulators, no verandahs for sun-bathing, no draughtless yet airy corner for cradles, no proper conveniences for bathing children, washing clothes, and keeping milk. We do all we can to discourage intelligent and energetic young women from early marriage and from having children. We dismiss them from their work; we intimidate them about their duty; we throw upon them the whole burden of domestic responsibility by teaching boys to think household occupations unmanly. Here in England we neglect maternity-services and leave it to the wife of an ex-prime minister to travel through the country pleading that the well-to-do should, of their charity, give money to provide chloroform to relieve the agony of childbirth. We seem far from the day when maternity is recognised as a benefit conferred upon the state rather than as an accidental handi-

cap laid by an all-wise Providence upon the weaker
sex.

So there are advantages in a proper respect for maternity.
But they are not adequate to compensate women for a lack
of respect for their humanity. The attempt to confine
women's interests to the function of motherhood alone is
as ill-proportioned a social enthusiasm as an attempt to
confine men's interests to fatherhood alone. It defeats its
own ends by making women less capable of successful
motherhood—which means much more than the physical
reproduction of healthy children. The danger in this
attitude lies in its element of compulsion, its emphasis upon
physical experience, its attempt to shape all women into
one mould. One effect is almost invariably—and perhaps
inevitably though irrationally—discouragement of birth
control. In Italy, under the Penal Code of 1931, advocacy
of contraceptive methods can be punished by imprisonment up to one year or a fine of up to 1,000 lire. The
penalties are even higher if the offender is a doctor or a
nurse. In Southern Ireland the rule of censorship is so
strict that English newspapers, even those of liberal views,
whose proprietors approve of birth control themselves,
often will not permit their contributors to mention contraceptive methods in their articles, since this would effectively
prevent any circulation of the Irish edition.

The right to choose her own time for her achievement of
maternity, the ability to plan her life and work, the freedom
from that accidental element which previously rendered
her an uncertain unit in social organisation, these consequences of scientific birth control have been perhaps the
greatest assets which modern civilisation has given to
women. But the cult of the cradle cancels them. It
suspects all freedom. It prefers the docility of the good
breeder and the fecundity of the good milch cow to the
capacity and companionship of a free human being, and
sacrifices the mother in one generation to the children who

may become mothers and fathers in their own. "Hammers producing hammers, producing hammers—and never a nail knocked in."

The Pope and Female Modesty

The quality of thought dominating both Fascist Italy and Southern Ireland is Catholic. Even where men and women are nominally agnostic or protestant, the social philosophy of Catholicism inevitably affects them in areas geographically or even historically influenced by the Holy See. The cult of the cradle is a feature not only of nationalism. It is a policy of modern Catholicism as it was a policy of ancient Hebraicism. Wherever a people, a church, a race or a cult believes itself to have been specially chosen by the Living God, it is its obvious business to increase and multiply until its seed covers the earth. Since Communism is wiping out Greek Orthodoxy quite effectively on its own, the Pope has only to prohibit all methods of birth control while Protestants and Agnostics are scientifically reducing their families, and then, by sheer force of numbers, Catholicism can recapture Christendom.

To-day Rome is fighting, in Western Europe and America, a stern and hitherto pretty successful battle. It is fighting against the claim of women to choose their own time and circumstances for conception, pregnancy and childbirth. It is fighting against the masculine attempt to escape the economic risk threatening satisfaction of passion. (The liability of imprisonment for non-payment of maintenance remains, for those to whom methods of contraception are prohibited or unknown, a rod in pickle for impetuous lovers.) It is fighting against the social experiment to control population by deliberate will and foresight rather than by the unpredictable orderings of an omnipotent Providence.

Catholic philosophy may have been ambiguous in former pronouncements about individual methods of averting conception. Its present policy of encouraging large families and discountenancing birth-control propaganda is unquestionable.

This matter is fundamental to women's position. But Catholic influence to-day does not end there.

When the Apostle Paul pronounced in his Epistle to the Galatians that in Jesus Christ there was no room for Jew nor Gentile, no room for male nor female, no room for bond nor free, he gave to the Christian Church its mandate of equality. That gospel of spiritual democracy still stands. But the social policy of Catholicism has followed a different model.

The Papal Encyclical upon Christian Marriage significantly entitled "Casti Connubii" and dated December 31, 1930, is a social document of immense importance. Naturally it upholds the view that matrimony is an indissoluble sacrament, divorce an unmitigated evil, birth control a sin, and the subservience of wives a divine principle.

The subjection of the wife to the husband, states the Encyclical, "does not deny or take away the liberty which belongs to the woman both in view of her dignity as a human being and in view of her most noble office as wife and mother and companion." But it does exclude that "exaggerated licence which is not for the good of the family" and it forbids that "in this body which is the family, the heart be separated from the head, to the great detriment of the whole body and the proximate danger of ruin."

The attitude is clear enough. In marriage the position of husband and of children is positive; that of the wife is dependent and ancillary.

After that theory of marriage it is logical that the Pope should warn his flock against "false teachers" who from "idle opinion" advocate the emancipation of women. Acceptance of their theories would not entail "true emancipation . . . nor that rational and exalted liberty which belongs to the whole office of the Christian woman and wife." This "false liberty and unnatural equality with the husband is to the detriment of the woman herself, for if she descends from her truly regal throne she will soon be reduced to her former state of slavery."

The reaction of the non-Catholic is to ask why there should be this inevitable alternation between throne and fetter. What is there about women that should force them to become either queens or slaves? The history of social evolution, the evidence of contemporary life, do not suggest this inexorable alternative. Why is there no room in the Catholic mind for comradeship and equality?

Again we are driven back to consider the origin of that fear which haunted Tertullian and which led even that artist of genius, Saint Augustine, to curious observations about the nature of women. To accept as authoritative the maxims upon marriage of a brilliant neurotic, whose own relationships to his mother, concubine and betrothed wife were far from exemplary and not even honourable, hardly inspires confidence in the non-Catholic observer. But the theory governing the Marriage Encyclical is not merely a legacy from Early Fathers.

In February 1934 the veteran Cardinal Bourne issued a Lenten Pastoral Letter to his English flock. In it he deplored "a kind of modernism which gives a certain toleration to departures from the traditional modesty reserve and reticence which are characteristic of Christianity," and he blamed particularly "the writers of books and painters of pictures, the actors on the stage and for the Screen, the women, by the fashion of their dress, who render self-control more difficult for the average normal man or woman."

It is the old cry of fear of the body, fear of the mysterious feminine power to disturb masculine equilibrium. The harsh breath from the desert that blew over pagan Africa to Imperial Rome stings with its fierce consciousness of danger through the prim restraint of the language. In the month when the Cardinal was writing, Europe, Christendom, indeed the whole world from West to East, were most gravely menaced by the threat of uncontrolled lusts and passions. The lust for power, the lust for possession, the lust for imposing opinion upon those who would resist it, were causing torture in Germany, bloodshed in Vienna, rioting in Paris, kidnapping and murder in the United States, conspiracy, hatred, fear and insecurity in every Christian country. There had rarely before been a profounder need for those values of mercy, courage, faithfulness and love preached by the Founder of the Christian faith. Yet the Cardinal expressed himself as chiefly concerned about the extravagances of women's dress.

It is this timid poking restlessness about the body, about sex, about modesty, about women as dangerous animals whose flesh must be hidden under ankle-length skirts and flowing sleeves in order to be rendered innocuous, that defaces Catholic Social theory. The superb metaphysic of its theological philosophy has little but dignity and reassurance to offer the human mind; but its nervous preoccupation with the body is inevitably disastrous to social sanity and explains the backwardness of women in every nation ruled by Catholic thought.

Freedom is not only a question of the law; it is a habit of the mind. To be free from the domination of the body is not possible to those afraid of it. Only when physical needs, feelings, actions and preoccupations become less important and less significant than intellectual and spiritual life, does the individual really escape from the "body of this death" which is mortality. The Catholic emphasis upon chastity, fidelity, maternity, and dignity destroys its own true object. Wherever in the modern world Catholic influence is in the ascendancy, women are subjected to this perpetual reminder of their sexual distinction, its dangers, its disadvantages and its precarious privileges. It is impossible that thus handicapped the majority of them should achieve full human maturity.

"*The March of the Women*"

The economic slump, the revolt against reason, the resurgence of military values, the cult of the cradle and the Catholic preoccupation with physical modesty—these are the chief forces which cause the pendulum of emancipation to swing backwards. Because reaction follows progress, they tend to affect countries like Germany, Great Britain, Ireland, and America where some advance had been gained more conspicuously than states like Italy and Spain which have never wholly deserted values dictated by Catholic influence.

But there is the other side. The forces of advancement are still active, and their effects appear in unexpected quarters.

The woman's movement, which arose at the end of the eighteenth century, is only now reaching in the less accessible countries the position from which the more "advanced" communities are now reacting.

Since 1918, fourteen states have written some form of equality of rights between the sexes into their constitutions: Austria, China, Dantzig, Esthonia, Germany, the Irish Free State, Latvia, Lithuania, Poland, Russia, Spain, Czechoslovakia, Ecuador and Finland. This constitutional affirmation may mean much or little. In Germany it has been already cancelled. In Ecuador it never meant more than a governmental gesture of modernity. An amusing travel book, *Interlude in Ecuador*, written by a young Canadian barrister, Janet Mackey, in 1933, gives an impression of social custom and conduct very far from any intimations of equality. In Spain as in Ireland the women are struggling between two influences.

The Spanish Constitution of 1931 carried in its Preliminary Chapter, Article II: "All Spaniards are equal

174

before the law." In Chapter III, Part I, Article 25 declared:
"Race, descent, sex, social class, wealth, political ideas or
religious beliefs shall not be considered the basis of privilege
in public law," and Chapter IV, Article 53, declared that
"all citizens over 23 years of age without distinction of
sex or civil status, shall be eligible for membership."

Spain to-day is in a state of flux. Its constitution is no
more sacrosanct than its ministries. These guarantees may
mean even less than the assertions of the British Sex Disqualification (Removal) Act of 1919. But it is something
that they have been made, and written into the fundamental
laws of a country notorious for its social subjection of
women.

It is true that Spanish women have frequently exerted
great individual influence. St. Theresa and Queen
Isabella are historical figures of dignity and power. When
in 1933 the Dominican nuns were forced to leave Spain,
it was remarked that one, Sister St. Paul, had been Professor
of French at Tarragona for thirty-two years. It is also true
that peasant women in Spain as in other countries could
prove formidable matriarchs, aggressively dominating village life. But in Spain as in other countries the behaviour
of the wealthier classes, the *bourgeoisie* and the aristocracy,
set the social standards, and there until the revolution, and
still to-day in most parts of the country, girls are educated
to be pawns in the family game of prestige and alliance,
submissive wives and fertile—if not particularly competent
—mothers. Their education is largely conventual; it is
limited and pious. Exquisite embroidery and the cooking
of elaborate dishes are thought more important items of
their curricula than hygiene, social science or elementary
economics, though these would, one might think, actually
serve them better even in their specialised destiny as housekeepers and mothers. Girls may not travel unchaperoned.
Courtship is a whole-time cult, yet marriage is usually
dictated by family interest. The *reja* through which com-

pliments are whispered, the mantilla employed as a veil to emphasise hidden charms, the parade to church where young men may be spied through interlaced fingers, notes dropped, and assignations made—these symptoms of semi-harem status are still observed in modern Spain.

But there are signs of another way of life. A few years ago the International Federation of University Women held its conference in Madrid and aroused great interest all over the country. Not only had Spaniards an opportunity of meeting distinguished women scientists, administrators, lawyers, writers, educationalists and technicians from other nations, but the visitors had the opportunity of meeting those Spanish women who have already escaped from behind the scroll-worked grill and become doctors, athletes, lecturers and organisers in their own country. In 1933 when women for the first time exercised their parliamentary franchise, five were elected as members of the Cortes. One girl, Margarita Sallavernia, passed fifteenth out of 270 into the Diplomatic Service, which is, in Spain, now open to women. Another, under the pseudonym of "Hildegart" established an astonishing reputation as lecturer and writer upon sociological subjects. When only seventeen she published studies of *The Eugenic Problem, Sexual Education* and *The Limitation of Offspring*, and gave lectures in crowded halls until this year her mother, in a tragic frenzy, killed her.

Two influences tug at every Spanish woman. The laws of property, the customs of society, the whole burden of tradition and prejudice, and the influence of the Catholic Church combine to stereotype the old position. But the leaven works. The equalitarian movement pulls the other way.

What has happened in Spain is not unique. The Latin Republics of South America had a tradition which, if not so rigid as that of Spain, was no more enlightened. Circumstance and the exigencies of pioneering communities broke down the habitual confinement of young girls except in the cities, but the Catholic influence there too tended to stereotype traditional manners. Recently, however, almost by accident, South American republics have vied with each other to encourage the international feminist movement. At Geneva, delegates for Chile or Venezuela have found the support or presentation of equalitarian resolutions a good opportunity for national advertisement, and what has been begun from one motive may sometimes be followed up from others. At the seventh Pan-American Conference at Montevideo the National Woman's Party of America, backed by women from the Southern Republics, was able to secure a treaty signed unanimously by the states-members, securing equal laws of nationality for all citizens of both sexes—a legal issue which is still being contested in Europe, where twenty or more different interpretations of nationality are accepted.

Among the fourteen countries which made constitutional declarations of equality between the sexes after the War, Norway, Sweden and Denmark were not included; yet it is there that—outside Russia—the principle of equality is most actively practised; nor was Holland mentioned, a country in which the woman's movement has progressed certainly as far as it did in England. Constitutional guarantees, are, after all, mainly symbolic.

The three Scandinavian states have pursued their own social evolution, aided by a harsh climate, a Protestant philosophy, and a natural vigour of temperament. The first made the kind of languorous sitting about and vapid flirtation of Southern countries less agreeable; the second encouraged independence of mind and freedom from the particular difficulties of Catholic philosophy; the third produced habits of social criticism which enabled artists like Ibsen to exercise so wide an influence. To-day we are apt to forget how revolutionary was his original exposure of the Dependent-Child-Wife in Nora Helmer, the Mother who-sacrifices-All-for-her-sons in Mrs. Alving, or the Lady-from-the-sea who, out of boredom and lack of proper responsibility, lost all contact with reality. In consequence Norway and Sweden have to-day perhaps the most enlightened social systems in the world. At international conferences the Scandinavian women are regarded as natural leaders. In July 1933 when the Open Door International held its conference in Prague, one delegate, Dagny Bang of Norway, reported how her government gave equal protection to workers of both sexes; and how in 1928 the Oslo Town Council had tried to discriminate against married women employees, but a vehement press campaign soon put an end to that. Consequently various minor evidences of social change appear in North-West Europe. For twenty years, for instance, in Hangesund two women have run a shipping firm of their own, consisting of six steamers amounting to 23,550 tons. They personally control repairs, engage their captains, and make their contracts. No one seems to judge their occupation strange. Without apparently thinking much about it they have as successfully broken the line between "women's interests" and "men's interests," as the English woman electrical engineer, Miss Jeanie Dicks, who secured the contract for re-wiring Winchester Cathedral.

This is old history. What is newer and more surprising is the evidence from further East, from the strongholds of the harem, of child marriage and sati. The news we receive is fragmentary and conditions obviously differ from place to place and individual to individual. Every sign of emancipation could be matched by twenty proofs of servitude; but opinion is stirring. Changes are coming more quickly than the West may realise.

For centuries, wherever Turkish dominion had touched Europe, those countries were notorious for their subjection of women. Mustapha Kemel Pasha in one year reversed Turkish policy; he discouraged the veil, the harem, the illiterate dependence of child wives. He introduced girl typists into government offices, and allowed "Miss Turkey" to parade unveiled in European Beauty Competitions. In 1933 an event of peculiar significance occurred. The municipality of Istambul abolished the two rows of curtained seats reserved in tram-cars for women. Henceforward they must sit with men and scramble for places as they may. They have become citizens and must accept the inconveniences as well as the privileges of equality.

In Iraq where Mahometan custom and thought are preserved with militant freshness, at the memorial service in 1933 to King Feisal, five hundred women came to mourn unveiled. Travellers from Palestine report that, in spite of the electrical hatred between Jews and Arabs, it is impossible to restrict all exchange of social influence. The veiled Arab women see the Jewish immigrant girls working beside their male colleagues. They hear stories of women doctors and agriculturalists. They see evidence of freedoms undreamed of, or previously condemned as impious and destructive. At Nahalal near Haifa is a farm run entirely by girls. News of this kind spreads quickly. There are reports of new activities in Persia. In 1933 the divorce laws, hitherto weighted hopelessly against wives, were reformed and made more equal. In Egypt, where the ruling caste is averse to social change, things are happening. A "Union Feministe Egyptienne" has been established. Hitherto its activities have been mildly philanthropic. But it received some government support for a dispensary which it has founded at Cairo. It is taking an active interest in education. In England, too, much of the woman's movement began in social philanthropy and school reform. In Egypt also, there has appeared the phenomenon of Mlle el Nadi Loutfia, an air pilot who, on December 23rd, 1933, won a day's round in the North African desert air race. Amy Johnson's flight to Australia exercised a considerable effect upon the imagination of young Englishwomen to whom the thought of women pilots was not new; the influence of Mlle el Nadi Loutfia on Egyptian girls must have been far more disturbing. In Cairo, too, there is an Evangelical Christian Mission college directed by an Englishwoman which trains Egyptian women to be preachers and evangelists.

Few psychological changes are so powerful as those which persuade people that they can do things of which they previously thought themselves incapable.

The changes in the Near East are mild compared with those in the Far East. We have taken for granted perhaps that when Burma sent delegates to discuss its constitution in London, they should include a woman; but Dr. Daw Saro Sa, medical practitioner and administrative organiser, is really a portent among Asiatic women. The Indian Franchise Act of 1919 gave provincial Legislatures power to enfranchise women on the same terms as men. That was revolutionary in theory; in practice it meant little, because the property qualification excluded all women but a very small minority—1 per cent. of adult females in Madras, .8 per cent. in Bombay, .3 per cent. in Bengal and only .2 per cent. in the Central Provinces. Over twenty men to one woman have the right to vote; women receive less education than men; the purdah system and the social if not physical martyrdom of widows persist; 322,000 of them are under fifteen years of age; and 126,000 Indian mothers die yearly in childbirth, many being themselves children of thirteen or little over.

But Indian women themselves are working to change these conditions. In 1917 the Women's Indian Association was founded in Madras; in 1925 the All India Women's Conference, and the National Council of Women in India. The constantly expanding membership of these organisations now runs into millions, and the views which they expressed and reported to the members of the Joint Select Committee on India's Constitution are anything but reactionary. They prefaced their report with the following remarks on "Fundamental Rights": "We strongly urge the necessity of the specific recognition of women's inherent right to full citizenship and equal opportunities with men for public service to the country. Therefore, in the declaration of Fundamental Rights, we wish it to be clearly stated that sex shall be no bar to any public employment, office, power or honour and in the exercise of any trade or calling." It is significant that in their comments on constitutional changes, these organisations strongly disapprove of the enfranchisement of wives and widows of persons possessing property qualifications, because "such a proposal is a direct negation of the woman's inherent right to citizenship." They want enfranchisement to be independent of the extraneous factor of marriage. "There exists a very strong feeling amongst the members of our Organisations who perceive that they, as women, are in themselves a vitally integral part of the body politic."

This is as clear an affirmation of the desire for equality as one could find in Europe. Nor is it an academic aspiration. The part played in the recent history of India by distinguished women, by Mrs. Besant, Mrs. Sarojini Naidu, Mrs. Metha of Ahmedebad, Mrs. Muthulakshmi Reddi, Mrs. Shareefah Hamid Ali, or Mrs. Kamala Nehru, demonstrate that Indian women can produce political leaders as able, as daring and as devoted as any in the more Western countries.

China presents equally violent extremes of evidence. We hear of a woman revolutionary general, organising her military staff, and of girl children sold by their parents into an "adoption" which is neither more nor less than slavery. At the Ginling College, Nanking, Chinese girls can receive a university education along the most advanced American lines, and through vast provinces a traveller might journey days and nights without encountering one literate woman. In the areas affected by Russian influence the doctrine of equality for Communist proletarians, without regard for sex or race, militates against the deeply engrained tradition of masculine domination.

The march of the women is never regular, consistent nor universal. It advances in one place while it retreats in others. One individual looks forward, another backward, and the notions of which is "forward" and which is "backward" differ as widely as the directions followed.

Moscow has a Plan

One country alone seems to have made up its mind about women's position. Evidence of what actually occurs in Russia may differ; opinions about its desirability violently disagree. But one thing is beyond contradiction. The communist theory has quite unambiguously stated the complete equality of status of men and women, and the Soviet Government has attempted with varying degrees of success to put this theory into practice. The rest of the world may march hither and thither along intersecting paths; Moscow has a plan.

The Plan seems the matter of chief significance. I have not been to Russia. Here as elsewhere I must rely upon travellers' reports and upon the statements of those who have created the U.S.S.R. Obviously experience varies. Russia is as much Asiatic as European. Until Peter the Great turned the eyes of his subjects westward, opened the terem, commanded that brides and bridegrooms should meet each other before marriage, forbade the use of the veil, and encouraged women to come to court and mix freely with his followers, conversing as though they were themselves human—an extraordinary innovation—Russia was little further advanced than Turkey when taken over by Kemal Pasha. Emperor and Dictator used the same brusque methods.

The eighteenth and nineteenth centuries saw the gradual education of aristocratic women, and a civilising of social habit; women took part in the liberal and revolutionary movements which followed, in 1861, the abolition of serfdom. Secondary schools were established, medical degrees gained, the professions entered. Krupskaya, Lenin's remarkable wife, served her apprenticeship to revolution in the Sunday Evening Adult Schools. The Women's Political Club of St. Petersburg became, early in the twentieth century, a rendezvous for political and social reformers.

But the great mass of the people remained ignorant, illiterate and superstitious, submitting to old traditions of wife-beating and masculine domination.

The communist thesis, as it was developed by the men and women who made the Russian Revolution, recognised no such masculine ascendancy. The people who counted were those members of the working class who accepted the Marxian thesis and revolutionary discipline. As the early Christians recognised in the Kingdom of Heaven neither male nor female, Jew nor Gentile, bond nor free, so the exiled revolutionaries imagined in their utopian republic no distinction of race, sex or nationality. Faith and works were in both cases the qualifications for citizenship.

"Without the women," wrote Lenin, "there can be no true mass movement." That is not so surprising a statement. Conservative members of parliament say no less to ladies of the Primrose League. Herr Hitler has said it about Germany. But Lenin went further. "It is our task to make politics accessible to every working woman," he said. To make politics accessible means to make education accessible, to make membership of political clubs and organisations accessible, to make authority accessible. "Very few men, even among proletarians, think how much labour and weariness they could lighten for women, in fact save them altogether, if they would lend a hand in 'women's work.' . . . We must root out the ancient order of the lord and master to the last fibre," he declared, in a letter to Clara Zetkin quoted by Fannina Halle in her book on *Women in Soviet Russia*. Now this seems going further still—going indeed to the very roots of the matter. For it is one thing to urge, as we have done in England, that women must be given education and opportunity to exercise it; it is another thing to suggest that those domestic responsibilities which still lay a double burden upon them should, as far as possible, be shared.

This is, I think, the great innovation of Soviet Russia. In its constitution, it offers no more than Latvia or Ecuador. In its social services, though its intentions reach further, its practice does not, I gather from the strange variety of evidence, compare favourably with what is offered in Holland, Czecho-slovakia, Great Britain or the United States. Russia is very proud of its clinics and hospitals, schools and maternity services, but Western capitalism could still probably give it points on these.

Where it leads the way completely is in the clarity of its position. Wherever it is possible to grant women equality simply by passing a decree, that has been done—in marriage, in divorce, in wardship, in property, in working conditions, in rules of citizenship. Further, wherever it is possible by law to carry that equality through to its logical conclusion, this is done. The most fundamental test of all, woman's right to bear her child when and where she chooses, and not to bear it even after conception, if she chooses, is not only recognised but made practicable. There is no legal penalisation of the child of unmarried parents. "The procreation of children," runs a decree of December 28th, 1917, "is a social function of women"— not *the* social function as the Catholic code implies, but a social function and one which must not be handicapped by artificial obstacles, by dismissal from work and by avoidable discomfort during pregnancy. Eight weeks' leave of absence are allowed before and after childbirth; a baby's outfit and "nursing allowance" is granted to every married woman on notification of childbirth. Pregnant women in industry may be put on lighter work but must not be dismissed or transferred from one factory to another without consent of the inspector. Nursing mothers are allowed to arrive an hour later at their work, and to have rest pauses for feeding their children, and no dismissal is supposed to be allowed within one year of delivery.

The system of crèches, gynæcological clinics and homes for mothers may be little better than those established elsewhere, though the figures of 130,000 ordinary crèches and 1,500,000 special harvest crèches in 1931 sound formidable. But the whole attitude of mind is new—that it is right for women to work, right for them to produce children, that the state is served equally by tractor drivers and by kindergarten teachers and that both may be mothers; that the state should encourage this double rôle as a service, and not discourage it as a dangerous and self-indulgent experiment—all this is surely new.

There are other innovations. In no other country has the attempt to abolish prostitution been so whole-hearted, nor, perhaps, so successful; though reports about the thoroughness of that success differ. Two commissions for combatting the evil have been appointed—one before and one after the institution of the New Economic Policy. In 1932 a circular recommended social and economic remedies for what has always been treated in Russia as an economic rather than moral evil. The circular suggested caution in dismissing women, the formation of co-operative groups for unemployed women, improvements of training, homes for destitute girls, vigorous measures against procuring and the whole business of exploitation, and better organisation of the treatment of venereal disease. Instead of Lock Hospitals, Russia has now Prophylacteria where girls are treated, not as social pariahs, but as disabled citizens who must be restored to health and competence as soon as possible. On the other hand the punishments for procuring, for rape, for forcing a woman into prostitution, or for infecting another person with venereal disease, are severe. In 1931 a conference was held which would hardly have been possible in any other country in the world. Marching in Red caps, with a brass band, came 150 "former prostitutes, now workers" to discuss their corporate problems under the chairmanship of the head doctor of the Moscow Prophylacteria.

Meanwhile within the party the range of vocational choice is as wide as possible. Women are encouraged to become engineers and agriculturalists as well as cooks and seamstresses, and they are given every possible chance of combining these occupations with wifehood and motherhood.

At the same time it is obvious that circumstances irrelevant to the theoretical plan of the government are having quite as strong an influence as any deliberate policy upon women's life in Russia. The urban housing shortage has contributed perhaps more than anything towards the disintegration of family life. It is not possible to cherish traditional sentiment about a "home" which consists of one room in a small flat populated by three or four families, whence all dwellers escape as quickly as possible, the adults to factories, clubs and communal dining-rooms, the children to schools, parks and crèches. When holidays are taken by individual ticket through a trades union or working club or school; when private hospitality is impossible owing to lack of money, food and room space; when "house-pride" has disappeared through lack of amenities of which one can be proud—then the lives of women are forcibly dragged out of their former shape.

And many dislike it. Beneath the reforming enthusiasm of convinced communists, the huge mass of the people obviously hug their ancient customs. Within the crowded towns that are being rushed so ruthlessly through their industrial revolution, there are thousands of women who sigh for the cosy, genial, friendly domestic life, for a hearth that was a family altar, ikons that guarded family worship, and meals that were family sacraments. Out on the great plains the peasant women cherish their immemorial superstitions. Sometimes they may hear of startling innovations. At Arlyuklinia in 1929 a hundred Cossack peasants founded a Woman's Commune, which has in this brief period grown to a community of 424 women and 254 men, controlling an area of 7,185 acres. A harvest crèche may be set up for the village during the hot summer work in the fields; schools may be built; a woman engineer may drive her lorry or tractor down the new roads. But a people so widely scattered, so heavily illiterate, so deeply impregnated with village tradition, does not alter its habits over night. There are plenty of Russian men and women to-day who vigorously resent these new "goings on" and do not hesitate to say so.

But what is important is the intention of the government and the direction in which all deliberate official action is taken. It is true that Lenin was succeeded by Stalin, not by a woman Tovarischi. It is true that among the members of the Moscow executive, women play no conspicuous part; that the general of the Red Army is a man; the ambassador to Great Britain is a man.

But the Soviet ambassador to Norway and Mexico has been a woman. There are women aviators in the Red Army and women officials in the Soviet trains.

The Soviet settlement has lasted only since 1917.

Since A.D. 17, since 1917 B.C., the older system held. Equality of status was neither dreamed of nor desired. Unfitted though most Russian men might be for authority when the Revolution came, the women were even more so. One must permit at least a few generations to pass before considering the scheme as a failure. At least it is a scheme—the first attempt to work out a way of life in which men and women shall have equal work, equal reward, equal responsibilities. Moscow has a plan.

The Conditions of Equality

Perhaps it is possible to generalise now with a little more certainty about the conditions of equality.

It is then always unfortunate when a new experiment is made under conditions which are, for extraneous reasons, themselves depressing. Let us presume that the slump is a temporary phenomenon, with all that it means of idle towns, nightly terror of dismissal, fear of blacklegging, and resentment against those girls who have undercut men and slipped into their jobs. After all, if this is not true—if the whole of Western civilisation is soon to be reduced to the conditions of Jarrow or Gateshead—the position of women is unenviable anyhow.

The first requisite would seem to be a rational philosophy of life. That is not as remote and high-falutin' a statement as it may appear. So long as we permit our nerves and instincts and traditions to over-ride our brains, our wills and our independent judgments, we shall be afraid to practise the disciplined experimentalism which the transition to equality demands. Wherever a civilisation deliberately courts its old memories, its secret fears and revulsions and unacknowledged magic, it destroys that candour of co-operation upon which real equality only can be based. The journey of mankind up from the slime of primeval forests has been a comparatively short one. We came trailing—not only clouds of glory—but dreads and hatreds and superstitions like jungle weeds. And those instinctive fears are reinforced by social and economic circumstance. The old dread of woman's magic power is added to the new dread of her industrial competition at lower wages. That fear gives to society the same strained watchfulness one finds also in countries where black and white or Jew and Gentile live in mutual distrust. One can hear to-day on verandahs of South African houses snatches of talk uncannily familiar: "The native has not the same obligations. His standard of life is lower. The native is only a child. He must be protected from political, or economic, or, as the case may be, social responsibility. This is no country for a White man." Or, "At least it's a white man's job." Substitute "woman" for "native," remove the "white" before "man," and the remarks fall into their habitual European character. The fear, the resulting contempt and mutual resentment are the same. Not all fears may be disastrous. There is the fear of the Lord which is, we are told, the beginning of wisdom. There is the fear of fate which is man's mortal heritage. But the fear of the thing we think to be inferior, the fear of the master for the slave, is a fear which scars the soul.

We must refuse to throw reason overboard.

Then we must preserve some kind of mechanical civilisation. It is perfectly true that the Industrial Revolution, controlled as it was by greed and complacency and short-sighted initiative, did as much harm as good. The black chards of decaying industrial towns tell their own tale of ruthless power and squalid confusion. But so long as men's bones and muscles have to perform what machinery now can do if we use it rightly, so long as tools are clumsy and navvy work essential, then muscle must count before quickness and intelligence and men must count for more than women.

Not that those callings in which men glory in their rough strength need disappear. The crews of North Sea trawlers may for generations boast of their power to keep at work night and day, without food on the slipping, ice-cold, pitching decks until they drop; agricultural labourers may still enjoy a day's forking till the tendons of their backs and thighs seem to swell and crack and the sweat rolls down their chests. But farms can be run, and boats too, by women if they choose to run them and to use their brains to save their muscle. That is the real test.

Thirdly, we must have effective and accessible knowledge of birth control. So long as women either are forced to remain celebate, or are unable to plan their lives because pregnancy may come upon them at any time, so long it is impossible that as workers or citizens they should be as reliable, as efficient, as regular as men. At the same time the woman's function of maternity must be recognised as a service to society, for which the community is prepared to make special conditions, and not purely as a female weakness which from time to time handicaps the woman worker.

Fourthly, I think that we must abandon military values. I am not so sure of this. For the sake of civilisation, I am convinced that it is necessary (just as we must overcome the economic slump. There is a war to-day down the mean streets of Tyneside and in the cotton towns of Lancashire, as there was in France in 1917—and it is devastating human lives). So long as we light-heartedly talk about national defence and increasing our air strength as though these were moves in an international football championship we are heaping up grim trouble for the children born to-day. We are spending on battleships what we need for bathrooms, on ammunition what we need for maternity centres; we are working for the destruction rather than for the preservation of human life. And that—for traditional and biological reasons, is work which does not appeal as much to women as to men. It may not always be so. But for the present, military values and the nationalist philosophy appear antagonistic to the equality of women.

And fifthly, we need greater elasticity in our political,

our economic and our social systems. We need to plan our civilisation so that our institutions leave room for individual difference. There is no reason why our statesmen should so grossly overwork their nerves and bodies while their minds atrophy among the political curiosities of of St. Stephen's, the Quai d'Orsay or Tammany Hall. There is no reason why millions of trained workers should loiter idle and wretched, while others, almost equally wretched from exhaustion, should toil for eight, nine, ten or more hours a day. In the adjustment which we shall soon have to learn—or perish—there should be opportunity for women who are mothers to work and to supervise their houses, just as there should be time for men who make motor-cars or quarry stones, at the same time to be gardeners, administrators, or second violins in the municipal orchestra.

We need, and we are, perhaps, beginning to achieve, greater elasticity in domestic organisation. There may one day be greater use of co-operation in domestic machinery and planning. There are women who love the snug individualism of their own back-yard, kitchen and parlour. Let them have it. There are others for whom the communal kitchen and restaurant—as in modern luxury flats— the professional cleaner with his electrical equipment, the crèche and nursery school, will solve a dozen at present apparently insoluble problems. Men may learn to take a larger share in household work, as they are learning to do in America, I understand. Spinsters will help in their spare time over-worked mothers, taking as compensation for the loss of their leisure, the tender and charming pleasures of bathing and feeding and amusing small children, and the enjoyment of returned affection.

It is no use asking for equality if it is not going to make us happier, wiser, more mature and vigorous human beings. When we talk about emancipation, it is as well to go a little further and ask—emancipation from what? What

191

are we to do with our equality when we have built a society in which it is possible to enjoy it?

There is the old story of the Chinaman at the Chicago Quick Lunch Counter who asked: "Now we have had quick lunch, what do we with time saved?"

I think that the real object behind our demand is not to reduce all men and women to the same dull pattern. It is rather to release their richness of variety. We still are greatly ignorant of our own natures. We do not know how much of what we usually describe as "feminine characteristics" are really "masculine," and how much "masculinity" is common to both sexes. Our hazards are often wildly off the mark. We do not even know—though we theorise and penalise with ferocious confidence—whether the "normal" sexual relationship is homo- or bi- or heterosexual. We are content to make vast generalisations which quite often fit the facts well enough to be tolerable, but which—also quite often—inflict indescribable because indefinable suffering on those individuals who cannot without pain conform to our rough-and-ready attempt to make all men good and happy.

It seems possible that in a wiser world we should walk more delicately. We might, perhaps, consider individuals as individuals, not primarily as members of this or that race, sex and status. We might be content to love the individual, perceiving in him or her a spirit which is divine as well as human and which has little to do with the accident of the body. We might allow individual ability rather than social tradition to determine what vocation each member of our community should follow.

And it is possible that in such a world we should find a variety of personality undreamed of to-day, a social solidarity to-day rendered unimaginable by prejudices, grievances, fears and repulsions, a radiance of adventure, of happiness and satisfaction now only hinted at by poets and prophets.

At least we know definitely enough whither the other ideal leads us. "We want men who are men and women who are women," writes Sir Oswald Mosley. He can find them at their quintessence in the slave markets of Abyssinia, or in the winding alleys of a Chinese city.

APPENDIX I

AUSTRIA. Women were granted the vote on the same terms as men on November 12th, 1918. They are eligible to sit for Parliament.

BELGIUM. Women are eligible to sit in the Senate and Chamber of Deputies and on Municipal Councils (1920-21). Only a limited number of women (war sufferers, etc.) have a Parliamentary vote, granted in 1919. They have municipal franchise on the same terms as men, granted in 1920.

BULGARIA. Women have no vote.

CZECHO-SLOVAKIA. Women granted equal suffrage and eligibility, February 29th, 1920.

DENMARK. Women granted muncipal suffrage in 1908, Parliamentary suffrage on June 5th, 1915; in both cases with eligibility.

ESTHONIA. After the war, when the Republic was declared, women were granted the same rights regarding franchise and eligibility as men.

FINLAND. Men and women have had equal voting rights since 1907.

FRANCE. Women have no vote.

GERMANY. In 1918 (November 9th) German women gained the right to vote and sit in Parliament. The former right they have retained, but under the present regime no women have been permitted to seek election to the Reichstag.

GREAT BRITAIN. Women gained the partial franchise with eligibility in 1918. On July 2nd, 1928, they received equal franchise with men.

GREECE. There is a limited measure of communal and municipal franchise, i.e. for women over 30 who can read and write.

HUNGARY. Women have a limited measure of franchise with a higher voting age than men and educational qualifications. They have the municipal franchise, with eligibility in some cases.

ITALY. Women have no vote.

LATVIA. Women were granted the franchise with eligibility when the independence of Latvia was proclaimed on November 18th, 1918.

LITHUANIA. Women were granted equal franchise with eligibility on August 1st, 1919.

NETHERLANDS. Women granted equal franchise with eligibility on September 9th, 1919.

NORWAY. Women gained the municipal franchise in 1910 and the parliamentary franchise in 1913.

POLAND. In 1918, after the departure of the Germans, the first Polish government gave women full political rights. On March 17th, 1921, these rights were written into the Constitution.

PORTUGAL. In 1931 the women of Portugal acquired a limited Parliamentary and Municipal franchise.

RUMANIA. In 1929 women obtained the municipal suffrage with eligibility subject to a number of restrictions. They have no parliamentary vote.

SPAIN. In 1924 a first measure of municipal franchise was granted to women heads of families. In 1931 the new Spanish Republic gave women equal suffrage with men, with the right to be elected to the Cortes.

SWEDEN. Swedish women acquired the municipal franchise in 1862. During the years 1862-1918 various other forms of franchise were granted them. In 1919 wherever the word "men" appeared in the Constitution, the words "men and women" were substituted. This change was ratified by Parliament in January 1921, thereby giving women equal suffrage rights with men.

SWITZERLAND. Women have no vote.

TURKEY. Although in 1923 a woman, the wife of Kemal Pasha, was elected to the National Assembly, in 1927 women became ineligible as members. In 1930 municipal franchise, with eligibility, was granted. Full electoral rights have been promised, but have not yet been granted.

U.S.S.R. Women have equal rights with men.

YUGO-SLAVIA. Women have no vote.

APPENDIX II.

1918. Affiliation Orders (Increase of Maximum Payment) Act.

1922. Criminal Law Amendment Act.

    (a) Raised age of consent in indecent assault from 13 to 16.

    (b) Took away plea of "reasonable cause to believe" that girl was over 16 except in cases of men under 23 and first offence.

    (c) Extended limit from 6 to 9 months in which action for criminal assault could be taken.

1923. Bastardy Act.

Raised maximum amount payable by affiliation order.

1923. Intoxicating Liquors (Sale to Persons under 18) Act.

Forbids sale to persons under 18 on licensed premises except where beer is sold with a meal. Forbids treating to young persons under 18.

1925. Widows, Orphans and Old Age Contributory Pensions Act.

Gives children's allowances:

    5s. for first child of widow.

    3s. for subsequent children.

    7s. 6d. for children if both parents dead.

1926. Adoption of Children Act.

Court has to be satisfied with circumstances of adoption.

1926. Registration of Midwives and Maternity Acts.

1926. Legitimacy Act.
>Legitimises children born out of wedlock if parents subsequently marry, provided that neither parent was married to another person at time of child's birth.

1929. Infant Life (Preservation) Act.
>Amends law with regard to destruction of children at or before birth.

1929. Age of Marriage Act.
>To raise age of marriage to 16 for both sexes.

1929. Children (Employment Abroad) Act.
>Extends protection of a 1913 Act to children up to 18.

1932-3. Children and Young Persons Act.
>Provides further protection of Children; regulates their employment, deals with juvenile delinquents.

SOME OF THE CAMPAIGNS CONDUCTED BY ENFRANCHISED WOMEN IN ENGLAND RESULTING IN REFORMED ADMINISTRATION

Save the Mothers Campaign—for the reduction of maternal mortality.

Infant Welfare Movement—for establishment of clinics under local authorities for ante- and post-natal treatment, advice on child welfare, etc.

National Association for the Prevention of Infant Mortality.

Nursery School Movement—for the education, welfare, health and remedial treatment of the pre-school child.

Birth Control Movement.

School Feeding Movement—for the provision of school meals or milk allowances to necessitous children.

Committee against malnutrition.

Children's Minimum Committee.

SHORT BIBLIOGRAPHY

Lady Fraser	*The Golden Bough* (Shortened Edition).
T. Briffault	*The Mothers.*
H. G. Wells	*Outline of History.*
Havelock Ellis	*Man and Woman.*
I. B. Horner	*Women under Primitive Buddhism.*
Edward Thompson	*Suttee.*
Margaret Smith	*Rabia the Mystic.*
	The Code of Hammurabi, King of Babylon.
G. Lowes Dickinson	*The Greek View of Life.*
F. A. Wright	*Feminism in Greek Literature.*
T. B. Allworthy	*Women in the Apostolic Church.*
Westermark	*A History of Marriage.*
John Langdon Davies	*A Short History of Women.*

Proceedings of the Sex Reform Conference, London, 1930

W. C. Lea	*The History of Sacerdotal Celibacy,* (3rd. Edition).
G. B. Shaw	*Saint Joan. Introduction.*
Bede Jarrett	*Social Theories of the Middle Ages.*
J. Eckenstein	*Woman Under Monasticism.*
Havelock Ellis	*The Task of Social Hygiene.*
Phillips M. Tomkinson	*English Women in Life and Letters.*
T. R. Smith (Compiled by)	*The Woman Question.*
Olive Schreiner	*Woman and Labour.*
Mary Wollstonecraft	*The Rights of Women.*
J. S. Mill	*The Subjection of Women.* Introduction by G. E. G. Catlin. (Everyman's Edition)

I. B. O'Malley	*Women in Subjection.*
W. F. Neff	*Victorian Working Women.*
Ray Strachey	*The Cause.*
Sylvia Pankhurst	*The Suffragette Movement.*
Barbara Drake	*Women in Trade Unions.*
War Cabinet Committee, H.M. Stationery Office	*Report on Women in Industry.*
J. Blainey	*The Woman Worker and Restrictive Legislation.*
Sylvia Anthony	*Women's Place in Industry and the Home.*
Sylvia Pankhurst	*The Home Front.*
Vera Brittain	*Testament of Youth.*
H. G. Wells	*The Work, Wealth and Happiness of Mankind.*
Maud I. Crofts	*Women under English Law.*
Virginia Woolf	*A Room of One's Own.*
Virginia Woolf (Edited by)	*Life as We have known it.*
Vera Brittain	*Women's Work in Modern England.*
H.M. Stationery Office	*Differentiation of Curricula between the Sexes in Secondary Schools*
G. B. Shaw	*Getting Married.*
Eleanor Rathbone	*The Disinherited Family.*
Sylvia Pankhurst	*Save the Mothers.*
Viscountess Rhondda	*Leisured Women.*
Cicely Hamilton	*Modern Russia.*
	Modern Germanies
	Modern France.
	Modern Italy.
Elaine Elnett	*Historic Origin and Social Development of Family Life in Russia.*

INDEX